Taekwondo

태권도

Taekwondo

THE ESSENTIAL INTRODUCTION

MARC TEDESCHI

Weatherhill

Taekwondo: The Essential Introduction

Copyright © 2003 by Marc Tedeschi

Published by Weatherhill Inc., 41 Monroe Turnpike,
Trumbull, CT 06611 USA. Protected by copyright
under the terms of the International Copyright
Union; all rights reserved. Except for fair use in
book reviews, no part of this book may be used or
reproduced for any reason by any means, including
any method of photographic or electronic repro-
duction, without permission. Printed in China on
acid-free paper meeting the ANSI Z39.48 Standard.

FIRST EDITION, 2003
First Printing

Book and cover design: Marc Tedeschi
Principal photography: Marc Tedeschi
Contributing photography: Shelley Firth,
Frank Deras, or as noted by photographs
Editorial supervision: Ray Furse
Korean language editing: Patrick Chew
Production consultation: Bill Rose
Printing and binding: Oceanic Graphic Printing
and C&C Offset Printing in China
Typeset in Helvetica Neue, Univers, Sabon,
Weiss, and Times on a Macintosh G4.
Other credits and acknowledgments
are found on the last page.

Library of Congress Cataloging-in-Publication Data
Tedeschi, Marc.
    Taekwondo: the essential introduction /
    Marc Tedeschi. —1st ed.
        p. cm.
    Includes bibliographical references.
    ISBN 0-8348-0537-5
    1. Taekwondo. I. Title
GV1114.9 .T42 2003
796.815'3—dc21   2003053789

Notice of Liability

The information in this book is distributed without
warranty and is only presented as a means of
preserving a unique aspect of the heritage of the
martial arts. All information and techniques are to
be used at the reader's sole discretion. While every
precaution has been taken in preparation of this
book, neither the author nor publisher shall have
any liability to any person or entity with respect
to injury, loss, or damage caused or alleged to
be caused directly or indirectly by the contents
contained in this book or by the procedures or
processes described herein. There is no guarantee
that the techniques described or shown in this book
will be safe or effective in any self-defense or sport
situation, or otherwise. You may be injured if you
apply or train in the techniques described in this
book. Consult a physician regarding whether to
attempt any technique described in this book.
Specific self-defense responses illustrated in this
book may not be justified in any particular situation
in view of all of the circumstances or under the
applicable federal, state, or local laws.

—

*For the real deal,
and all those who
embrace, nourish,
and sustain it.*

—

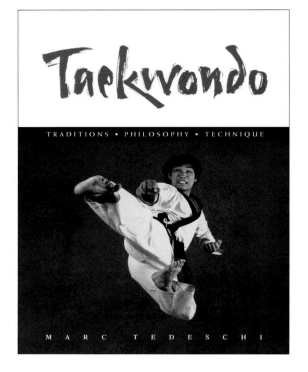

This book is intended to provide readers
with a brief overview of Taekwondo,
the world's most widely practiced
martial art and sport, and to give
novice students essential guidance during
their first several months of training.
Readers seeking a comprehensive
presentation of the art should
consult the author's 896-page work,
Taekwondo: Traditions, Philosophy, Technique,
which is shown above (ISBN 0-8348-0515-4).
For further information, please call
Weatherhill at 800-437-7840 or visit
www.tedeschi-media.com

CONTENTS

How This Book is Organized
In order to help the reader comprehend the large amount of material which defines Taekwondo, this book is organized into seven parts:

Part 1 is a brief overview of history, philosophy, and technique.

Part 2 is a brief overview of some of the more important basic technical elements that define Taekwondo.

Part 3 shows how basic skills are combined for practical self-defense. Twenty techniques are shown in detail. They are a representative sample drawn from hundreds of Taekwondo techniques.

Part 4 is a very brief overview of Olympic-Style sport competition and shows 8 typical techniques. They are a representative sample drawn from over 140 typical sparring techniques.

Part 5 is an overview of principles and skills used in breaking demonstrations.

Part 6 is a brief overview of major forms used by different Taekwondo styles.

Reference material includes information on rank advancement, important Korean terms, and sources for further reading.

Editorial Notes
The following editorial conventions have been adopted for use in this book: To avoid sexist grammar, *they, them, their,* and *themselves* are used in place of the singular pronouns *he, she, him, her, his, hers, himself,* and *herself.* To avoid wordiness, articles are sometimes omitted from captions and technical descriptions, and abbreviations are employed, specifically: (R) for right, (L) for left, (cw) for clockwise, and (ccw) for counterclockwise. Personal names are written English-language style, given name followed by surname. The names of specific techniques are capitalized.

INTRODUCTION

Overview

Since its beginnings in the mid-twentieth century, Taekwondo has experienced phenomenal growth and undergone dramatic changes in its technical repertoire. This has led to great diversity in how the art is practiced and defined. Although many books have been produced over the years, virtually none portray the art in its totality. This absence of comprehensive literature, coupled with a lack of honest, accurate, nonpoliticized information, has led to widespread misunderstanding about exactly what Taekwondo is, and is not.

In April 2003, the most definitive work ever written on Taekwondo was published under the title, *Taekwondo: Traditions, Philosophy, Technique*. This 896-page work contains more than 8600 photographs, documents over 700 core techniques, and has been widely acclaimed for its comprehensive integration of traditional and modern approaches, sport and self-defense, in a single text. Nonetheless, not everyone needs, wants, or can afford such a substantial book on the subject. Consequently, this smaller introductory book has been written by the same author, to provide a brief overview of Taekwondo, and to give novice students basic material to assist them during their initial months of training.

Although this book has been based on its 896-page predecessor, it is important to recognize that no book consisting of several hundred pages can ever hope to accurately document Taekwondo in its entirety. To study a martial art in a serious manner means to study it in its entirety—its history, philosophy, and technique. Some aspects of Taekwondo can be learned from a book; however, there is much that can only be learned by direct experience, and by training for years under a qualified master. A quality book can amplify this process, but it cannot replace it. Serious martial artists seeking a more comprehensive understanding of Taekwondo are urged to buy the larger work, on which this book is based, and to train in a serious, dedicated, and joyful manner. For in the end, it is the quality and frequency of one's training that matters most.

What is Taekwondo?

Taekwondo is a Korean martial art which emerged in the mid-twentieth century, and has subsequently become one of the most widely practiced martial arts in the world. The art is characterized by powerful hand strikes and kicks, which are used for unarmed self-defense or combat, or in organized sport competitions such as the Olympic Games.

Like many Asian martial arts, Taekwondo emphasizes the unification of mind, body, and spirit; the perfection of human character; social responsibility; and the appropriate use of force. Thus, practicing the art involves both mental and physical training.

From a technical standpoint, Taekwondo primarily focuses on fast, powerful, kicking and punching techniques, which are blended with sophisticated footwork, jumps, blocks, and avoiding actions. In recent years, some Taekwondo styles have begun to incorporate a limited number of joint locks, throws, and ground defenses into their curricula, to keep pace with the needs of modern society and the reality of contemporary self-defense. Internal-energy development is not emphasized to the degree it is in many soft-style martial arts, but is still a fundamental part of training, leading to increased health and greater efficiency in martial techniques. Generally speaking, Taekwondo's core techniques (particularly kicks) have evolved based on modern scientific principles, and Western anatomical and biomechanical concepts of the human body. Many of the more modern innovations have been driven by lessons learned in sport competition.

In contemporary society, Taekwondo is practiced by men, women, and children of all ages, for reasons encompassing self-defense, physical fitness, sport competition, artistic expression, and character development. It is estimated that there are more than 50 million Taekwondo practitioners worldwide. Since 1988, Taekwondo has been included in the Olympic Games, which has contributed to its phenomenal growth and popularity.

Taekwondo's Structure

Today there are many different styles of Taekwondo being practiced. Nonetheless, one finds certain core activities that are common to virtually all. While Taekwondo may be organized or articulated differently by different systems, most styles generally encompass five core activities, upon which the structure of this book is based:

- Practice of Fundamentals
- Self-Defense
- Sport Sparring
- Breaking
- Forms

These five core activities are intended to have both combat value and to help practitioners evolve physically, mentally, and spiritually. In actual training, all activities are interrelated. None is more important than the other, and all are mutually interdependent, constituting an indivisible whole. For example: fundamental skills, such as punches, kicks, and blocks, are ingrained through constant repetition of basic motions. These skills are further refined by practicing prearranged patterns of movements and techniques (called *forms*), against imaginary opponents. Speed and power are further refined and tested by attempting to break various materials. Lastly, techniques are further developed through various forms of sparring (self-defense or sport), in which the student must now interact with a real opponent. This builds improvisational skills, footwork, and a realistic sense of combat.

It is important to understand that these five activities are not related to one's rank or experience, nor do they occur in any particular order or sequence. The training of both the master and the novice will be defined by these five activities throughout their training careers, although their focus is obviously quite different. For example, masters will constantly return to the *practice of fundamentals* to maintain and refine, and to practice an activity that they have come to love and enjoy; whereas the novice practices fundamentals to learn and ingrain basic skills.

Practice of Fundamentals (Kibon Tallyŏn)
The practice of fundamentals involves mental and physical training in individual techniques, such as kicks, punches, footwork, and stances—the basic elements that compose Taekwondo. Training usually involves constant repetition of basic motions in order to ingrain skills and perfect technique. This can involve a range of activities, such as target kicking, repetitive drills to perfect specific strikes, breathing exercises, flexibility exercises, and meditation. The practice of fundamentals can be done individually or in unison with one's classmates. Fundamental skills are further refined through sparring (self-defense or sport), breaking, and forms practice.

Self-Defense (Hoshin)
This activity involves training in specific unarmed techniques designed to protect oneself or others. Fundamental skills are combined and refined in a realistic context that attempts to approximate actual combat. This can involve *prearranged sparring*, in which trainees perform predetermined actions; or *free sparring*, in which trainees must learn to spontaneously improvise based on the changing dynamics of combat. Generally, sparring is an essential activity for developing free-thinking skills, footwork, and a realistic sense of combat.

Sport Sparring (Shihap Kyŏrugi)
The purpose of competitive sport sparring is to: 1) hold a contest of skills based on specific rules in which the competitors and spectators can enjoy the act of winning and losing; 2) provide a forum in which one can test and develop skills, with less risk of injury than real combat permits; and 3) provide an activity that promotes the cultivation of positive moral values and character qualities that are an essential part of other aspects of life—qualities such as inner strength, resiliency, confidence, assertiveness, and the ability to triumph over adversity, accept defeat graciously, and never give up. There are many different forms of sport sparring, ranging from full-contact Olympic-Style to no-contact point fighting. Like the previous activity (*self-defense*), training can involve prearranged or free sparring. Historically, *self-defense* and *sport sparring* were conceptualized as a single activity called "sparring" (*kyŏrugi* or *taeryŏn*). Today, these two activities are so vastly different, it is more helpful to consider them separately.

Breaking (Kyŏkp'a)
In this activity, the Taekwondoist attempts to break different materials—such as wood, bricks, tiles, and granite—by using specific striking techniques. Breaking techniques, often noted for their spectacular effect, are not practiced to impress people, but to perfect crucial aspects of striking, such as proper hand/foot formation, speed, power, penetration, timing, accuracy, concentration, breathing, and mind-body-spirit harmony. Breaking also provides a socially acceptable forum for practicing deadly, full-power blows.

Forms (Hyŏng, P'umsae, or T'ŭl)
Forms are specific solo exercises in which the Taekwondoist practices a predetermined, continuous pattern of movements and techniques, against imaginary opponents. Forms are used to ingrain basic motions and combinations; develop speed, fluidity, timing, power, endurance, and proper breathing; sharpen concentration; and build conditioned responses to various forms of attacks and counterattacks. One of the advantages of forms training is that it does not require a partner and can be practiced anywhere there is sufficient space. Forms are graded in terms of their difficulty and are usually selected based on one's skill and rank. The specific sets of forms being practiced today vary widely, depending on the style of Taekwondo one practices. Many forms have historical or philosophical concepts associated with them.

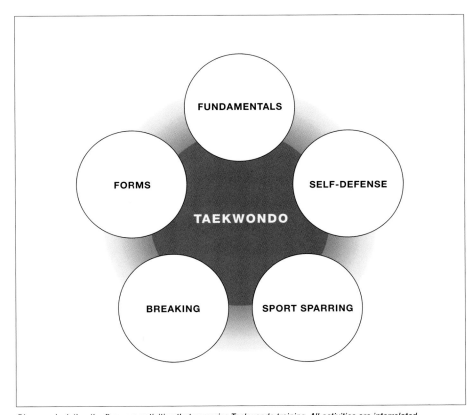

Diagram depicting the five core activities that comprise Taekwondo training. All activities are interrelated. None is more important than the other, and all are mutually interdependent, constituting an indivisible whole.

Martial arts, like people, are imbued at the moment of their birth with an essential structure which will define the remainder of their existence. In a person, this is called one's "true nature." It is that fundamental set of qualities that makes something wholly unique unto itself, like no other. Understanding our true nature is essential, since it helps us determine the course of events which allow us to grow and prosper. For martial artists, understanding the roots of their style is vital, since the roots define the art, determining the

HISTORY

manner by which the art will grow and evolve over time. For novices, a sense of history gives them a connection to the past and to a tradition greater than themselves, while for masters, a sense of history is crucial if they wish to be a vital part of a living, evolving martial art, such as Taekwondo. A collective understanding of Taekwondo's origins, philosophy, and techniques thus allows us to build on its foundation in a way that permits diversity of expression, while retaining those essential qualities that make it only Taekwondo.

The Evolution of Martial Arts

The history of the martial arts is essentially an oral tradition. Very little was actually written down until recent times. When one begins examining a broad range of martial arts, it becomes quickly evident that much of their history is contradictory. It is not uncommon to find a particular martial art tracing its roots to the "dawn of time." Specific histories are often touted as fact when they may be little more than anecdotes, or a loose collection of unsubstantiated myths.

The history of most martial arts are intimately entwined with those of the civilizations and cultures with which they are associated. Some ancient cultures left written or visual evidence, others did not.

Fighting skills have of course existed since the dawn of time and developed concurrently in many different geographic regions. These early skills, used by primitive humans for hunting and self-protection, eventually evolved into more sophisticated martial arts. As the modes of travel and communication evolved, cross-cultural influences and wars allowed neighboring societies to observe and absorb martial skills from outside sources. Buddhism, an important element in Korean, Chinese, and Japanese cultures, is known to have originated in India and subsequently spread throughout Central, East, and Southeast Asia. Many Buddhist and Taoist monks practiced martial arts and transmitted their ideas and techniques across cultures.

The earliest written evidence of specific empty-hand arts appears in Egypt, Greece, Crete, and India, although it is likely indigenous martial systems existed in other areas as well. It is thought that the migration of martial arts from China and India to neighboring regions influenced the development of native arts throughout Asia. Among the arts emerging between 400 and 1650 are: Aiki-Jujutsu, Bushido, Capoeri, Chin Na, Chinese Boxing, Jojutsu, Kenjutsu, Kung Fu, Nen Ryu, Ninjutsu, Silat, Subak, Sumo, Tai Chi Chuan, Te, Yawara, and Win Chun.

Taekwondo's Roots

"Taekwondo" is a coined word originally created in 1955 to unify a broad range of Korean hard-styles that evolved from native Korean arts. The evolution of these earlier hard-styles was also influenced, in varying degrees, by contact with Japanese and Chinese martial arts encountered during frequent national conflicts in the first half of the twentieth century. As a result, many early Taekwondo styles exhibited distinct similarities with Chinese and Japanese martial arts.

During the latter part of the twentieth century, Taekwondo changed dramatically as its philosophical and technical foundation evolved, mostly as a result of Korean efforts to purge overtly foreign influences, incorporate new technical innovations, and reframe the art in a manner that more fully reflected Korea's culture, traditions, and national character. While Taekwondo has often been characterized in the past as a Korean interpretation of Japanese Karate—which many feel it was in its infancy—there can be little doubt today that it has evolved into a unique martial art that is very much a product of Korean culture, just as Japanese Karate evolved from its earlier Chinese roots according to the needs of Japanese culture.

Taekwondo's evolution from a derivative style into a unique martial art and global sport did not occur overnight, and not without strife and discord within its own ranks—growing pains that continue even today. In order to fully understand the dynamic circumstances surrounding Taekwondo's evolution, its roots, and the source material from which its technical foundation developed, one must trace the evolution of both Korean and foreign martial arts. Such an exercise also reveals Taekwondo's relationship to other twentieth century arts such as Tang Soo Do, Karate, Kempo, and Korean eclectic styles such as Hapkido, Kuk Sool Won, and Hwa Rang Do.

Wall painting depicting empty-hand fighting. Ceiling of Muyong-Chong tomb, AD 3 – AD 427, Three Kingdoms Period.

Early Korean Arts

The Korean peninsula was first inhabited around 30,000 BC, when nomadic tribes from Central and Northern Asia migrated into the area. The earliest outside influences absorbed by these tribes likely came through contact with the Chinese, who established commanderies (outposts) in the northern part of the Korean peninsula, from around 108 BC. Constant wars with the Chinese forced these scattered tribal settlements to gradually coalesce into larger political entities, eventually leading to the formation of three powerful kingdoms: Koguryŏ, Silla, and Paekche. This marked the beginning of the Three Kingdoms Period (18 BC – AD 668).

During this period, Korean arts, architecture, literature, politics, and military arts flourished, as Chinese influences continued to be assimilated and reinterpreted in a uniquely Korean manner. Buddhism gradually became the state religion of all three kingdoms, and was eventually transmitted to Japan by way of Paekche. Increasing contact between the cultures of Korea, Japan, and China not only influenced their respective societies, but their native martial arts as well.

Native Korean martial arts are thought to have first emerged sometime during the Three Kingdoms Period (18 BC – AD 668). During this time, Korean martial arts did not possess a single umbrella-name. Instead, it is believed that specific skills were grouped into technique areas, which were labeled using generic terms. Some of these terms are:

Su Bak	(punching and butting)
T'ae Kyŏn	(kicking)
Kag Ju	(throwing)
Kung Sa	(archery)
Ki Ma Sa Bŏp	(horse archery)
Tan Gŏm Sul	(short-knife)
Kŏm Sul Bŏp	(sword skills)
Su Yŏng Bŏp	(fighting in water)

Note that these are not the names of specific martial arts styles or systems, although they are often used incorrectly in this context.

While it has been recorded that martial arts training was taken seriously and contests were popular, there are unfortunately no surviving written accounts describing these native martial systems or their specific techniques. The limited information we do have comes mostly from paintings, artifacts, and two ancient Korean manuscripts: the *Samkuk Saki* ("Three Kingdoms History"), written in the twelfth century, and the *Samkuk Yusa* ("Three Kingdoms Memorabilia"), written in the thirteenth century. Ancient Chinese and Japanese texts also make occasional reference to Korean martial arts.

It was during the Three Kingdoms Period that two notable warrior classes evolved: the *Sun Bi* ("intelligent-brave"), and later, the *Hwa Rang* ("flower of youth"). The Hwa Rang emerged in the Silla kingdom about 550. In addition to being warriors, they are reputed to have established a high moral code of conduct and were schooled in the intellectual and cultural arts of the time. They were later instrumental in unifying Korea and are also thought to have influenced development of Japanese Bushido ("way of the warrior"), a code of ethics followed by the Japanese warrior-classes. This early transmission of

Korean peninsula during Three Kingdoms Period (18 BC – AD 668). Maps courtesy of the Victoria and Albert Museum.

Korean martial arts may have occurred during the Three Kingdoms Period, when Korean culture was first exported to Japan. For example, architects from Korean Paekche were heavily involved in the proliferation of temple building which occurred in Japan during the sixth century. In fact, there were times during Japan's early history when there were more Koreans involved in secular and religious positions than Japanese.

The Korean peninsula was first unified in 668 when the Silla kingdom conquered Koguryŏ and Paekche. This unification would last through various changes in governments until the mid-twentieth century. For the next 800 years, Korean martial arts went through various periods of advance and decline, depending upon the prevailing political climate and the needs of the people. Around 1100, the generic term *Yu Sul* ("soft arts") emerged as an umbrella term for a range of soft-style martial skills. Yu Sul is said to have

been characterized by throws (mechigi), grappling (kuchigi), and attacks to vital points (kuepso chirigi). Kuepso Chirigi is the Korean equivalent of Japanese Atemi and Chinese Tien Hsueh and Dim Mok—all of which were integrated into many contemporary arts.

Sometime after 1400 more sophisticated empty-hand fighting systems evolved. Kwŏn Bŏp ("law of the fist") emerged as an umbrella term for Korean empty-hand techniques. Ssirŭm was a system of grappling skills, with roots in Mongolian wrestling. Pakchigi was a system of head-butting,

popular in northern Korea. Kag Sul and T'ae Kyŏn were systems emphasizing kicks, and Su Sul was a system of empty-hand techniques derived from sword skills. At some point, Kag Sul eventually came to be called T'ae Kyŏn, and Su Sul to be called Subyukta. Subyukta has also been referred to as Su Bak, Su Bak Ki, and Su Bak Do. T'ae Kyŏn was widely practiced and continued to evolve into the twentieth century. Many of the philosophical ideas and martial techniques found throughout these systems, would eventually be integrated into Taekwondo and other modern Korean martial arts.

Korean Chronology

Scholars and historians generally define Korean history according to the following time periods.

Neolithic	c. 4000 – 1000 BC
Bronze Age	c. 900 – 400 BC
Iron Age	400 – 200 BC

Division between North and South

Chinese Commanderies	108 BC – AD 313
Three Han States	0 – AD 200
Mahan	
Chinhan	
Pyŏnhan	

Three Kingdoms	
Koguryŏ	37 BC – AD 668
Paekche	18 BC – AD 663
Early Silla	57 BC – AD 668

United Silla	668 – 935
Koryŏ	935 – 1392
Chosŏn (Yi Dynasty)	1392 – 1910
Japanese Colonial Period	1910 – 1945

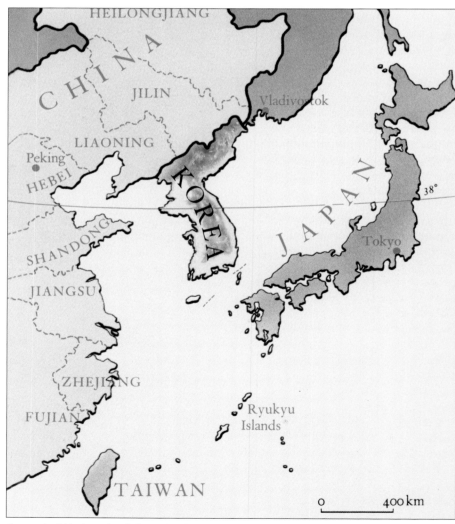

Korea and neighboring regions before 1945. After 1945 Korea was partitioned into North Korea and South Korea.

Early Chinese and Japanese Arts
There are various theories concerning how the hard-style martial art we have come to call *Karate* evolved. One commonly held view is that Chinese martial skills (*Ch'üan Fa*) were first exported into the Ryukyu archipelago (now part of Japan) sometime between 600 and 1200, most likely by early Chinese expeditions, or when survivors fleeing from Japan's tenth-century feudal wars swarmed into the Ryukyu islands, particularly Okinawa. Some historians believe that these imported arts subsequently mixed with native Okinawan arts, called *Tode* ("Chinese hand"). After 1350, Okinawa began to develop rapidly, largely as a result of diplomatic relations with China, Korea, and Japan, and trade with neighboring regions, including Taiwan, Siam, Malacca, Sumatra, and Java. Martial arts from these regions were likely introduced during this time, and may have been freely mixed with Chinese Ch'üan Fa and native Okinawan skills.

In the early 1600s, the Japanese invaded Okinawa, subsequently banning the practice of martial arts and the possession of many weapons. As a result, empty-hand systems were studied secretly for the next several hundred years, and over time, modified according to the needs of the Okinawan people. These techniques came to be referred to using various terms, most commonly *Te* ("hand"). Sometime between 1780 and 1903,

when Okinawa was being assimilated into the Japanese cultural sphere, Okinawans adopted the name *Karate* ("Chinese hand") to replace "*Te*." "Kara-te" is a coined word combining two characters: *Kara*, the ideogram for the T'ang Dynasty of China; and *Te*, the ideogram for "hand." By 1910, this name was in widespread use throughout Okinawa. Notable Okinawan styles ("*ryu*") at that time include: Goju-ryu, Kan-ryu, Kushin-ryu, Nihon Kempo-ryu, Shindo Jinen-ryu, Shorin-ryu, Shotokan-ryu, and Wado-ryu.

Beginning around 1915, Okinawan Karate was adopted by the Japanese, who gradually modified it according to their own needs, strengthening it with skills found in Japanese Jujutsu (empty-hand combat systems) and Atemi (attacks to vital points). The most obvious differences between the Okinawan and Japanese styles were that the Japanese favored a more linear or angular approach, whereas the Okinawan styles utilized quick, circular motions that were more similar to Chinese styles. *Karate-do* ("Chinese-hand way") and *Karate-jutsu* ("Chinese-hand art") are other commonly used terms that emerged in the early twentieth century.

In the mid 1930s, the ideogram for Kara ("Chinese") was changed to an ideogram meaning "empty" (as in emptying oneself to achieve serenity)—also pronounced as "Kara." The use of an alternate character for

"Kara" began as early as 1906, but did not become standardized until the mid 1930s. Japanese masters made this change to distance themselves from Chinese arts, reflect the fact that their newer art was a product of Japanese/Okinawan innovation, indicate the art was an empty-hand system, and signal that mental and spiritual qualities were also an important part of training. By the mid twentieth century, Karate had evolved into numerous global styles.

The Birth of Taekwondo
From the 1890s to 1945, Korea was involved in frequent conflicts with and between China and Japan. During this period, many Koreans learned extensively about martial arts being practiced in these countries. As a result, many foreign skills were fused into native Korean martial arts. Tang Soo Do ("Chinese-hand way"), Kong Soo Do ("empty-hand way"), Su Bak Ki ("hand striking technique"), and Tae Soo Do ("foot-hand way") were some of the twentieth century hard-style arts that resulted and later evolved into Taekwondo.

In 1910, the Japanese annexed Korea, abolished the Korean monarchy, and outlawed all Korean martial arts. During this time many Koreans studied Japanese Jujutsu, Judo, and Kendo while continuing to practice native martial arts in secret. It is thought that Korean monasteries may have played an important role in preserving many of the native arts.

"Chinese Hand"
The Chinese characters meaning "Chinese hand" or "hand of the Tang Dynasty" are shown above. In Chinese they are read as "T'ang Shou," in Korean as "Tang Soo," in Japanese as "Kara-te" or "To-de."

"Empty Hand"
The Chinese characters meaning "empty hand" are shown above. In Chinese they are read as "K'ung Shou," in Korean as "Kong Soo," in Japanese as "Kara-te" (same pronunciation as left example).

"Law of the Fist"
The Chinese characters meaning "law of the fist" or "fist rules" are shown above. In Chinese they are read as "Ch'üan Fa" (Mandarin) or "Ken Fat" (Cantonese), in Korean as "Kwŏn Bŏp," in Japanese as "Kempo."

In the following decades, in the face of continued public unrest and intermittent guerrilla activity, Japanese rule became progressively more brutal. Censorship tightened, the teaching of Korean history and culture was banned, the Japanese language was made mandatory instruction in all schools, and all public signs were required to be in Japanese. As World War II approached, hundreds of thousands of Korean laborers were drafted to assist the Japanese Army in Korea and China—essentially slave labor. Most Koreans view this 36-year period as one of attempted cultural genocide, in which an entire generation lost its freedom and cultural identity. Even today the scars are evident.

Korea after 1945
In 1945, World War II ended and Korea regained its independence from Japan. Many Korean masters who had been living in China and Japan returned to Korea, bringing with them extensive martial training in foreign styles. The post-war period was an extremely fertile time for Korean martial arts, as many traditional styles were being rediscovered and synthesized into new eclectic styles. Many martial arts that had been practiced in secret for decades were being taught publicly for the first time, as various masters vied for public recognition. In decades to come, younger Korean martial artists would also attempt to rediscover and reorganize traditional martial skills into new comprehensive systems that would preserve their national character and prevent them from becoming extinct.

Tang Soo Do, Kong Soo Do, Su Bak Ki, Kwŏn Bŏp, and Tae Soo Do were some of the names that came to represent the different styles that preceded Taekwondo. Some historians believe that many of these systems were essentially Japanese Karate, which was subsequently fused with reemerging native Korean techniques, particularly kicks. There were also masters who claimed to be teaching older forms of Korean T'ae Kyŏn, most notably Dok-Ki Song (1893–1987). Some martial historians cite T'ae Kyŏn as a major influence on Taekwondo, while others think it unlikely given their technical dissimilarities. Some of the hard-style schools (called *kwans*) that emerged between 1944 and 1955 are listed in the table below, along with their founding head master and initial martial style(s).

Many associations were formed in the two decades following World War II, in an attempt to unify Korean hard-styles under a single umbrella. However, differences in philosophy and politics, and rivalries among the various schools, made unification impossible. Many of these early associations were short lived, as various factions repeatedly merged and split apart. Some of the early Korean associations were: the Taehan Kong Soo Do Association ("Korea Empty Hand Way"), formed during the Korean War (1950–1953); the Taehan Subak Do Association ("Korea Hand-Strike Way"); and the Taehan Tae Soo Do Association (Korea Foot-Hand Way"), formed in 1961 and later renamed the Korea Taekwondo Association

Early Hard-Style Kwans

Date	School Name	English Translation	Head Master	Style Taught	Location
1944	Ch'ŏng Do Kwan	"Blue Wave School"	Wŏn-Kuk Lee	Tang Soo Do	Seoul
1944	Song Mu Kwan	"Pine Tree School"	Byŏng-Jik Ro	Tang Soo Do, Kong Soo Do	Kaesŏng
1945	Mu Dŏk Kwan	"Martial Virtue School"	Kee Hwang	Tang Soo Do	Seoul
1946	Ch'ang Mu Kwan	"Martial Development School"	Byŏng-In Yun [3]	Kwŏn Bŏp, Kong Soo Do	Seoul
1946	Yŏn Mu Kwan [1]	"Yŏn Martial School" [2]	Sang-Sŏp Chŏn [1]	Kwŏn Bŏp, Kong Soo Do	Seoul
1953	Chi Do Kwan [1]	"Wisdom Way School"	Kwae-Byŏng Yun [1]	Kwŏn Bŏp, Kong Soo Do	Seoul
1953	O Do Kwan	"My Way School"	Hong-Hi Choi	Mix of hard-styles	Korean Army

Note: Founding dates are approximate. "Style taught" indicates the style name(s) commonly associated with a school; however, everything was in constant flux with allegiances and names constantly shifting. "Location" is the place where school first opened. Many of these early schools met in leased temples, YMCA's, or other temporary facilities.
1) Yŏn Mu Kwan founder, Sang-Sŏp Chŏn, disappeared during the Korean War. His successor, Kwae-Byŏng Yun, renamed the school "Chi Do Kwan" around 1953.
2) "Yŏn" is an abstract, coined term of undetermined meaning. Perhaps it is meant to suggest the Korean words "Yŏng" ("spirit" or "soul") or "Yŏnggu" ("continuing" or "eternal").
3) Ch'ang Mu Kwan founder, Byŏng-In Yun, was missing-in-action during the Korean War. His successor was Nam-Suk Lee.

in 1965. "Tae Soo Do" was one of the names initially favored as a new umbrella name for Korean hard-style martial arts (c. 1953).

In April 1955, a meeting was held between various masters, historians, and political leaders, at which time "Taekwondo" ("foot-fist way") was proposed as a new umbrella name for all Korean hard-styles. Proponents favored the name for its descriptive qualities, its phonetic similarities to " T'ae Kyŏn," and its "Korean-ness," which they felt inspired a sense of cultural pride and nationalism. By the mid 1960s, most hard-style schools had adopted the new name, although a few did not—most notably some of the Tang Soo Do systems, which continue to use the name "Tang Soo Do" to this day (Note: the Mu Dŏk Kwan evolved into two distinct systems: Mu Dŏk Kwan Tang Soo Do and Mu Dŏk Kwan Taekwondo).

Disputes and friction between the various Taekwondo schools and associations continued throughout the 1960s, with many schools staunchly opposing unification. Two of the dominant associations that emerged in these years, the Korea Taekwondo Association (KTA) and the International Taekwon-do Federation (ITF), were at irreconcilable odds over a variety of issues ranging from the integration of Taekwondo forms to the authority to control Taekwondo's international growth. In 1972, General Hong-Hi Choi, founder and head of the International Taekwon-do Federation (and a former president of the KTA), left South Korea, allegedly as a result of political problems stemming from a controversial goodwill trip he made to North Korea. This resulted in the ITF headquarters being moved to Toronto, Canada. Ultimately, with government intervention and the ITF out of South Korea, the Korea Taekwondo Association won out in the bid for power, resulting in the formation of the World Taekwondo Federation (WTF) in 1973, with Un-Yong Kim as president.

By late 1970s, the name Taekwondo was commonly in use and the style was considered a major Korean martial art, with formal government recognition. Eventually, many Taekwondo masters emigrated overseas and established the art globally.

During the 1980s and 1990s, sport Taekwondo experienced phenomenal growth, largely as result of the WTF's efforts. In 1988, Taekwondo became a demonstration sport at the 1988 Seoul Olympic Games. It remained a demonstration sport (except for 1996) until the 2000 Sydney Olympic Games, at which time it became a permanent Olympic event.

Currently Taekwondo is not unified under a single international federation. The World Taekwondo Federation (WTF) in South Korea is the largest association, claiming more than five million black belts worldwide. The International Taekwon-do Federation is also well established globally, but split into two organizations in 2002, as a result of internal politics. There are many other associations and national governing federations, both in the United States and around the world. Currently, the WTF estimates that there are more than 50 million Taekwondo practitioners in over 167 countries, making Taekwondo likely the most widely practiced martial art. A more detailed history, with historical photos, charts, and martial genealogies, can be found in the author's 896-page Taekwondo book.

Taekwondo written in Korean characters (Han'gŭl): top is "T'ae," center is "Kwŏn," bottom is "Do."

Wall painting likely depicting empty-hand fighting between two warriors. Anak tomb, AD 3 – AD 427, Three Kingdoms Period. Although often cited as evidence of Su Bak, the precise meaning of the warriors' postures remains uncertain.

A martial art's philosophical system defines the moral and spiritual values embraced by its practitioners, and determines the manner in which the art is practiced, including technique preferences. The technical differences between most martial arts are defined by the unique ways in which they use and combine martial skills. This is largely determined by matters of philosophy, as the techniques themselves are often very similar. Taekwondo philosophy is an outgrowth of East Asian philosophy, which has historically been defined by

PHILOSOPHY

Buddhism, Taoism, and Confucianism. Many East Asian martial arts share similar roots, and therefore, distinct philosophical similarities. The following pages briefly outline the fundamental concepts embraced by virtually all Taekwondo systems. It is not necessary for one to have a background in Asian philosophy to understand these concepts; however, it will lead to a deeper understanding of the inherent relationship between all martial arts. Some suggestions for further reading can be found at the end of this book.

Taekwondo's Purpose

Taekwondo's essential purpose is abstractly expressed in the meanings and symbolism associated with its name. *Taekwondo* is a Korean word coined from three separate word-concepts: T'ae, Kwŏn, and Do. In the Korean language, *T'ae* means "foot," *Kwŏn* means "fist," and *Do* means "the way," "method," or "path." Therefore, the name Taekwondo literally means "foot-fist way" or "the way of the foot and the fist" or "method of the feet and hands." On a more symbolic level, *Taekwon* refers to Taekwondo's physical nature; that is, a martial art whose primary tools are the fist and the foot. Taekwondo's philosophical nature is suggested in the incorporation of the term "do." *Do* connotes a way of life, or a path that one follows, which is in harmony with the universe.

Fundamental Beliefs

A fundamental belief of Taekwondo is the idea that martial arts training is a way of life (*do*), one which embraces intense mental and physical training focusing on the growth and harmonization of one's physical, mental, emotional, and spiritual centers, in order to cultivate *correct and instantaneous action*. This means that one will do the right thing at the right time without hesitation, and can refer to physical, moral, or spiritual matters. For example: avoiding a deadly blow, timing a strike, expressing gratitude, coming to the aid of another, or offering assistance. Correct and instantaneous action is expressed as an intuitive response to life, unfettered by mental deliberations or self doubt—the proper action is instantly perceived and acted upon.

In our society, a person who demonstrates instant correct action is often characterized as a person of integrity, or one who possesses inner strength, courage, nobility of character, and a strong altruistic sense of purpose. In combat, instant correct action is manifest as reflex reactions that are perfectly timed and morally appropriate to the situation. Instant correct action can only truly occur when one's physical, mental, emotional, and spiritual centers operate as one. This harmony

within leads to harmony with the outer world. Grandmaster Hong-Hi Choi stated this quite eloquently, when he described Taekwondo as a way to "bring about the flowering of morality, beauty, and power in harmony with the immortal spirit."

Moral Values

Taekwondo's moral values are similar to the values stressed throughout society as a whole, and evolved from various philosophical and religious traditions. While specific written listings often vary among different Taekwondo styles, there are five basic tenets that have been adopted by many, which evolved from older moral precepts commonly associated with Korea's ancient warrior societies. These modern principles, typically referred to as the *Tenets of Taekwondo*, are:

- Courtesy   *Yeŭi*
- Integrity   *Yŏmch'i*
- Perseverance   *Innae*
- Self-Control   *Chaje*
- Indomitable Spirit *Paekjŏl Pulgul*

Courtesy

Courtesy is most nobly embodied by acts that demonstrate a deep enduring respect and consideration for the rights and feelings of others. In the martial arts, courtesy is much more than polite manners or gallantry; it is a reflection of a deeper sense of compassion and caring for things larger than oneself. When one is possessed by a high regard for the greater good, courteous acts do not require a deliberate effort, but become a natural expression of one's inner state.

Integrity

In the martial arts, integrity is demonstrated by knowing the difference between right and wrong, and always attempting to do the right thing, regardless of the consequences to oneself. This means accepting blame for one's mistakes, feeling guilt, and attempting to put things right when possible. Integrity is difficult to attain, but is easily traded away. Once you lose it in the eyes of others, it is very difficult to recover.

Perseverance

No goal worth attaining can be achieved without perseverance. In the martial arts, perseverance is most nobly demonstrated by a steadfast, enduring determination to stay the course, regardless of discomfort, physical or emotional pain, or feelings of failure, fear, or self-doubt. The ability to persevere and overcome great obstacles and challenges can only come from a strong inner resolve, a belief in oneself, and a confidence in one's intimate and unalienable connection to the greater universe. Unwavering courage, fortitude, patience, and mental and physical resiliency are all underlying character traits that are integral to the ability to persevere.

Self-Control

Self-control is the ability to exercise restraint over one's impulses, emotions, or desires. Without self-control, the practice of martial arts is an extremely dangerous activity. A loss of self-control during sparring can easily result in serious injury to oneself or partner. When one loses self-control, one is no longer in harmony with oneself or the outside world. In combat, this is a recipe for defeat; in life, it leads to failure and an alienation from other human beings. Judicious self-control is fundamental if one hopes to evolve toward a seamless unification of body, mind, and spirit. In its highest form, self-control is far more than a mere reflection of self-denial or discipline; it is the embodiment of patience, tolerance, and a profound respect for life and for oneself.

Indomitable Spirit

All great acts of courage and heroism in the face of overwhelming obstacles are ultimately a reflection of indomitable spirit. In the martial arts, the cultivation of indomitable spirit is considered to be centrally important. It is most nobly manifest in those individuals whose principles and resolve cannot be broken, subdued, conquered, or defeated. In its highest form, indomitable spirit is the reflection of a bedrock morality, unassailable convictions, and an unconquerable spirit—irrespective of victory or defeat.

Taekwondo training is a way of life that embraces intense mental and physical training focusing on the development of one's body, mind, and spirit in harmony with the universe.

PHILOSOPHICAL UNDERPINNINGS

There are several important concepts expressed throughout East Asia that are at the root of its philosophies, religions, and culture. These concepts postulate a basic orientation toward life and being, from which many subsequent martial theories evolved. Generally, an understanding of East Asian philosophy is more important in Eastern medicine or energetic-oriented martial arts, such as Hapkido, Tai Chi Chuan, and Aikido. While the influence of these East Asian concepts is less evident in Taekwondo, they nevertheless remain an important underpinning that influences one's approach to life and the practice of Taekwondo.

Universal Law (Tao)

Tao (*Do* or *To* in Korean) literally means "way" or "path." It is the ultimate law governing the workings of the universe. Yet the Tao is not "law" in the literal sense—a canon of "how things work" and "how to act." Rather, it is more like a natural order that binds and embraces all things, in a very loose sense comparing to the Christian concept of "God." It is said that the meaning of Tao cannot be adequately expressed in words or symbols, but that these merely give us a sense of its spirit. This spirit is well expressed in the following quotation from the philosopher Lao Tzu in the Chinese classic *Tao Te Ching*:

There is a thing inherent and natural,
Which existed before heaven and earth.
Motionless and fathomless, it stands alone and
never changes; It pervades everywhere and
never becomes exhausted. It may be regarded
as the mother of the Universe. I do not know
its name. If I am forced to give it a name,
I call it Tao, and I name it as supreme.
Supreme means going on; going on means
going far; going far means returning.
Therefore Tao is supreme; heaven is supreme;
earth is supreme; and man is also supreme.
There are in the universe four things supreme,
and man is one of them. Man follows the laws
of earth; earth follows the laws of heaven;
heaven follows the laws of Tao;
Tao follows the laws of its intrinsic nature.

Law of Change (Yin-Yang)

The East Asian concept of change postulates that all transformation occurs by the constant interplay of two universal primal states of being. They were first called *the firm* and *the yielding,* and later expressed as *yang* and *yin* (*yang* and *ŭm* in Korean). Yang, the firm (depicted by an unbroken line ——), and Yin, the yielding (depicted by a broken line – –), symbolize the two great forces at play in the universe. These forces exist in all things, in a state of constant tension and balance. One defines the other and each contains within it the seed of its opposite; one in essence but two in manifestation, always in flux. In Eastern thought, yin-yang forces of change can be seen operating in natural cycles such as day and night, winter and summer. Typical correspondences are listed at the lower right.

The yin-yang symbol, called the *Tai Chi* in Chinese (meaning "supreme ultimate"), depicts the two great forces in perfect balance and perpetual alteration, with yang becoming yin, and yin becoming yang; each possessing within itself the embryo of the other. This well-known symbol represents the perfection of balance and harmony, and the creative union of opposites throughout the universe. It is widely represented throughout Asian art and culture and is even incorporated into national symbols, such as the South Korean flag.

The illustration at lower-left shows the Tai Chi (*T'aegŭk* in Korean) surrounded by the eight trigrams symbolizing the primary combinations of yin and yang forces (note: the top of each trigram faces outward; the numbers are added and correspond to the key below). The eight trigrams (*Bagua* in Chinese, or *P'algwae* in Korean), were conceived as symbols of all that happens in heaven and on earth, and represent the nature of changing transitional states. Each trigram consists of a unique combination of yin and yang lines, and are classified as described in the illustration. For those wishing to engage in further study, these concepts are outlined in the classic Chinese text, the *I Ching*. This 3000-year-old book of wisdom is one of the *Five Classics of Confucianism* and provided the common source for Confucian and Taoist philosophy.

Tai Chi Symbol + Trigrams

	Trigram Name	Attribute	Image
1	the Creative	strong	heaven
2	the Receptive	yielding	earth
3	Keeping Still	resting	mountain
4	the Joyous	joyful	lake
5	the Arousing	movement	thunder
6	the Gentle	penetrating	wind
7	the Clinging	light-giving	fire
8	the Abysmal	dangerous	water

Yin-Yang Correspondences

Yin	Yang
Earth	Heaven
Female	Male
Night	Day
Moon	Sun
Low	High
Heaviness	Lightness
Falling Tendency	Rising Tendency
Movement inward	Movement outward
Relative stasis	Clear action
Interior	Exterior
Front	Back
Lower section	Upper section
Bones	Skin
Inner organs	Outer organs
Blood	Ki
Inhibition	Stimulation
Deficiency	Excess
Yielding	Firm
Essence	Spirit

Triple Essence (Samjae)

Samjae is a Korean concept rooted in ancient cosmology, which postulates that the universe is defined by three fundamental essences: *heaven*, depicted by a circle (○); *earth*, depicted by a square (□); and *human being*, depicted by a triangle (△). The principle of *Samjae* is represented in the *Samt'aegŭk* ("Triple Supreme Ultimate"), an ancient East Asian symbol embraced by Korean culture, which represents the constant interplay of these three fundamental essences (heaven, earth, and human), with three becoming one and one becoming three. In this aspect of Korean philosophy, the mind and body are inseparable within a human being, a human being is inseparable from heaven and earth, and heaven and earth are inseparable from each other. Thus, heaven, earth, and human being are destined to exist in unity. The human being becomes a micro-universe that links to the larger universe to become a single entity. Samjae is essentially a concept revolving around the process of transformation or change, not unlike that expressed in yin and yang, as outlined previously.

Universal Life Force (Ki)

The primal forces of yin and yang are often collectively referred to as *Ki* in Korean or Japanese, or *Qi* or *Chi* in Chinese. The word itself is essentially untranslatable, although it is often described as the "vital energy" or "life force" that permeates the universe, flowing through and animating all things. It is the basis of Eastern medicine and many healing arts. In ancient thought, Ki was said to give the world substance, through its manifestation in the *five phases* of the universe—wood, fire, metal, water, and earth (also called *the five elements*).

Ki's Role in the Body

The human body is viewed as a complex network of *meridians,* which are pathways distributing Ki throughout the body, vitalizing cells, tissue, organs, and other systems. The meridians have been traced and diagrammed for centuries in numerous Asian cultures, including in Tibet, India, China, Korea, Japan, Thailand, Malaysia, and Indonesia. Alternating states of wellness or illness are said to result from a balance, imbalance, or blockage in one's Ki or internal energy. As a result, humans have attempted to manipulate Ki-flow for centuries through visualization, breathing, physical intervention, or meditation. This is reflected in such disciplines as acupuncture, massage, yoga, and internal martial arts.

At this time, mainstream Taekwondo is primarily an external oriented martial art. Thus, internal energy development is not a focus of training in most systems, unless a particular master makes it so. Ki training is more emphasized in internal oriented arts such as Tai Chi Chuan, Hapkido, and Aikido. This does not mean that a Taekwondoist cannot add Ki training to their training regime if they wish. Many masters do exactly that, primarily by engaging in a serious meditation practice or a Ki Gong system. "Ki Gong" ("internal energy cultivation") is a generic term used to represent a range of systems that focus on meditation and movement to cultivate Ki and promote health and longevity. Ki and its role in martial arts is discussed in much greater detail in author's book *Essential Anatomy for Healing and Martial Arts*.

Samt'aegŭk symbol depicting interplay of heaven, earth, and human being (often in blue, red, and yellow)

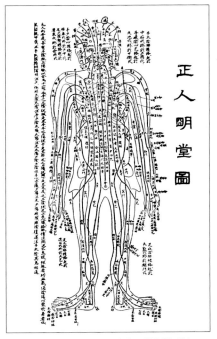

Drawing depicting the flow of Ki, c. 200 BC, China

TECHNICAL PRINCIPLES

Today there are a many different styles of Taekwondo being practiced. Nonetheless, one finds certain core technical principles that are common to all. While these principles may be expressed differently in different styles, they generally involve the following key concepts:

- Evolution through Science
- Concentration of Power
- Balance
- Breath Control
- Mastery through Repetition

Evolution through Science

Because Taekwondo evolved in the modern era, its masters have placed a strong emphasis on the use of modern Western scientific principles as a basis for evolving technique. This typically involves the application of physics, biomechanics, and nutrition. Having a basic grasp of these disciplines can help the Taekwondoist to better understand why their techniques work, why they fail, and how they can be improved.

The application of these principles can also lead to a reduction in injuries and increased health and well-being. In sport Taekwondo, a constant evaluation of physics, biomechanics, nutrition, and lifestyle factors is extremely important, since minute technical refinements or increases in body performance often make the difference between winning and losing.

The Physics of Power

The force of a blow at impact is mostly dependent upon the limb's velocity, weight, and muscle force, and the surface area of the portion of the limb making contact. All other factors being equal, a strike using a small hitting surface (e.g., the knuckles) will create more force at impact than a strike using a large surface (e.g., the palm). Generally, the two most variable factors are *velocity* and *muscle force.* Consequently, most physical training focuses on: 1) developing musculature in order to increase speed and strength, and 2) perfecting biomechanical motions to maximize the efficiency by which velocity and muscle force are produced.

Concentration of Power

Taekwondo, like many hard-style martial arts, focuses on producing maximum power by using the entire body to support a strike, and by focusing force at the smallest point. The use of one's entire body is characterized by simultaneous coordinated motions of the limbs, shoulders, and hips, which are designed to increase speed and transfer power to the striker's hitting surface. Generally, the striker's body moves in a fluid, relaxed manner that becomes explosively focused at the moment of impact, with the muscles becoming momentarily tensed, then immediately relaxing to initiate the next action. This constant relaxing and tensing of the body's musculature is what allows one to produce maximum power without losing speed and fluidity. The constant muscle tension often seen in novices increases reaction time, greatly diminishes both speed and power, and leads to a stiff, sluggish, ineffectual manner of fighting. Generally, this excess tension disappears as fear dissipates and one gains experience and athleticism.

The proper use of physics, concentration of power, breath control, and the total commitment of one's body, mind, and spirit is shown during a breaking demonstration.

Balance

Historically, Taekwondo's martial techniques have been executed from strong, balanced postures with the trunk erect and the center of gravity in the hips. This *rooted* posture was designed to keep one from being unbalanced or knocked down by the force of one's own blow, or a blow one was hit by. When moving between postures, one's center of gravity would rise during the step, then sink down as one again adopted a stationary posture, usually while delivering a block, punch, or kick. Today, the development of intricate footwork, and fast, fluid strike combinations has caused Taekwondo's traditional concepts of *rooted* balance to shift toward a more mobile conceptualization, where balance is a dynamically changing state integrated with constant motion. This shift is mostly the result of innovations occurring in Olympic-Style Taekwondo. In self-defense, rooted concepts may still be relevant at times, particularly if facing a grappler. In this scenario, the Taekwondoist must avoid being thrown, since their ground skills are negligible.

Breath Control

In Taekwondo, controlled breathing is used to maximize the body's performance, leading to increased speed, power, and endurance, and more focused concentration. Breath control is also used during strikes and blocks to help coordinate and time the body's actions, so power is focused at the moment of impact. Proper, well-timed breathing can also be used to increase the body's resistance to the effects of forceful blows to vital points. Breath control techniques will be explained more fully in Part 2, under *Breathing + Meditation*.

Mastery through Repetition

Historically, in hard-style martial arts there is an old adage: it takes three years to learn to properly clench a fist, another three years to learn proper balance and posture, and lastly, three more years to learn how to strike. Why so long? Striking requires correct formation of one's hitting surfaces, a strong foundation (posture), good balance, proper weight transfer, correct use of the hips and shoulders, and well-timed, efficient, precise biomechanical actions. These skills are not obtained overnight, but rather through the experience of constant, dedicated, repetitive practice over a long period of time.

In today's world, many people come to expect instantaneous results, which they have been led to believe are obtainable through quick-and-easy programs, technology, by reading books, or by spending enough money. While many modern innovations and methods of teaching can accelerate training time, there are unfortunately few shortcuts to mastery in the martial arts. If you want to acquire the skills and benefits that martial training provides, you can only achieve this through the direct *experience* of serious, dedicated, *repetitive* training. Constant repetition deeply ingrains biomechanical motions and physical responses that are essential to performing at the highest level. Only through constant repetition can you refine, simplify, and build the auto-responses that are essential to making smooth, intuitive transitions in self-defense, combat, or sport competition.

Mastery of technique can only occur through the experience of regular repetitive practice over a long period of time. In this photo, Taekwondoists practice basic motions in unison.

All techniques observed within the martial arts world can be organized into seven basic categories: striking, avoiding and blocking, holding, throwing, weapons, internal techniques (meditation, breathing, internal energy development), and healing. The differences in technique between most martial arts are defined by the unique manner in which they use or combine one or more of these seven technical categories. The art of Taekwondo, which focuses on the first two categories, is characterized by powerful hand strikes and kicks,

TECHNIQUE OVERVIEW

which are used for unarmed self-defense or combat, or in organized sport competitions such as the Olympic Games. Generally speaking, Taekwondo's core techniques, particularly kicks, have evolved based on modern scientific principles. The following pages provide a brief technical overview of Taekwondo in its entirety. This is how the art is commonly structured, and is reflected in the organization of this book. All of these techniques are documented in detail in the author's 896-page Taekwondo book.

TAEKWONDO TECHNIQUES

The following outline summarizes Taekwondo's major techniques by category. It is not meant to be a complete listing of all techniques or an indication of teaching methodology, but rather to provide a general overview of the physical techniques that define mainstream Taekwondo.

Breathing + Meditation

Various forms of breathing and meditation are used to enhance physical performance, focus the mind, increase concentration, and improve health. Specific techniques vary from system to system.

Warmups

Taekwondo training includes extensive warmup exercises used to heat up the body, and increase one's flexibility, range of motion, power, speed, endurance, agility, and aerobic capacity. The author's 896-page Taekwondo book contains more than 50 typical exercises.

Stances

Taekwondo makes use of about 28 basic stances as a platform for launching techniques. In this book, they are divided into four categories:

- Natural Stances
- Fighting Stances
- Special Stances
- Olympic-Style Stances

Movement

Taekwondo predominantly focuses on stand-up fighting; therefore, footwork is vitally important. Taekwondo movement is characterized by stepping, sliding, running, jumping, turning, and spinning, and basic methods of falling (called breakfalls), which are designed to protect oneself from injury. There are about 40 basic forms of movement divided into three categories:

- Basic Steps
- Combination Steps
- Breakfalls

Targets

Taekwondo strikes, kicks, and blocks focus on attacking the body's vital points, which consist of about 90 anatomical targets. Taekwondo identifies these targets by using the modern scientific terms of Western medicine. For training and combat purposes, the human body is divided into specific target zones, called *sections* and *lines*. The most basic division yields three horizontal sections: *High Section* (area above shoulders); *Middle Section* (area between shoulders and navel); and *Low Section* (area below navel). *Midline* refers to a vertical line intersecting the solar plexus. *Chest Line* refers to a vertical line intersecting the chest nipple. *Shoulder Line* refers to a vertical line intersecting the shoulder joint.

Attack Points

These are the specific parts of your body you will use to execute specific techniques. In some Taekwondo styles, they are called *tools*. There are about 40 basic body surfaces used for striking, kicking, and blocking. This usually involves specific formations of the hands and feet (e.g., a clenched fist).

Striking Techniques

Taekwondo striking techniques use about 40 basic body surfaces to deliver blows. There are more than 100 basic strikes, with numerous variations. They are classified as:

- Hand Strikes
- Elbow Strikes
- Jump Hand Strikes
- Standing Kicks
- Knee Strikes
- Jump Kicks
- Jump Combination Kicks
- Jump-Over Kicks
- Special Kicks
- Ground Kicks

Combination Strikes

Multiple strikes can be executed sequentially or simultaneously (e.g., punch and kick at the same time). There are an infinite number of possible combinations.

Avoiding + Blocking Techniques

Blocking techniques use the hands, arms, and legs against all forms of strikes. In some traditionally oriented systems, blocking skills are learned before striking skills. There are about five basic avoiding movements and 86 basic blocking skills, with numerous variations. They are classified as:

- Avoiding Techniques
- Forearm Blocks
- Hand Blocks
- Two-Hand Blocks
- Leg Blocks
- Pull-Outs
- Special Postures

Grappling Techniques

Grappling skills (joint locks, chokes, throws, ground fighting) are not traditionally part of Taekwondo, although many schools are adding this material. The specific techniques being adopted varies widely by school, system, and federation. In most cases, these techniques are not a significant part of training, and therefore have not yet been integrated into Taekwondo's repertoire in a seamless manner. Rather, they are grafted appendages borrowed from other martial arts, most notably Hapkido. Consequently, this material will not be presented in this text. Grappling has been covered extensively in four other books by this author: *The Art of Holding*, *The Art of Throwing*, *The Art of Ground Fighting*, and *Hapkido: Traditions, Philosophy, Technique*.

Self-Defense

For teaching purposes, self-defense skills are generally practiced in the context of *prearranged sparring*, in which trainees perform predetermined actions; and *free sparring*, in which trainees must learn to spontaneously improvise based on the changing dynamics of combat.

Olympic-Style Sparring

Olympic-Style sparring is a sophisticated, global competitive sport. A variety of highly specialized training procedures are used including calisthenics, target kicking, prearranged sparring, and free sparring.

Breaking

Taekwondoists practice a wide range of breaking techniques, using a range of strikes to break different materials, such as wood, bricks, tiles, and granite. Breaking is widely used in demonstrations and during testing.

Forms

Taekwondo as a whole consists of many different sets of forms. The specific forms being practiced varies widely, depending on the style of Taekwondo one practices. Regardless of style, all sets of forms are graded in terms of their difficulty, and are usually selected based on one's skill and rank. The 49 forms selected for inclusion in the author's 896-page Taekwondo book are those most widely observed today in mainstream Taekwondo. These forms are organized into four categories:

• P'algwae
• T'aegŭk
• WTF Black Belt Forms
• ITF Patterns

There are numerous other sets of forms that are practiced in specific styles, such as the *Kich'o* ("foundation") series, *Kibon* ("basic") series, and *Pyung-Ahn* series.

Technique Nomenclature

Technique names in this book are based on commonly used terms, and are rendered in both English and Korean in the author's 896-page book. However, within Taekwondo there still remains a great deal of variability in term use. Different terms are frequently used to represent the same technique. Whenever possible, the clearest or most commonly accepted nomenclature is used in this text. The appendices at the back of the 896-page Taekwondo book contain a cross-index of technique names as used by major styles (in English and Korean).

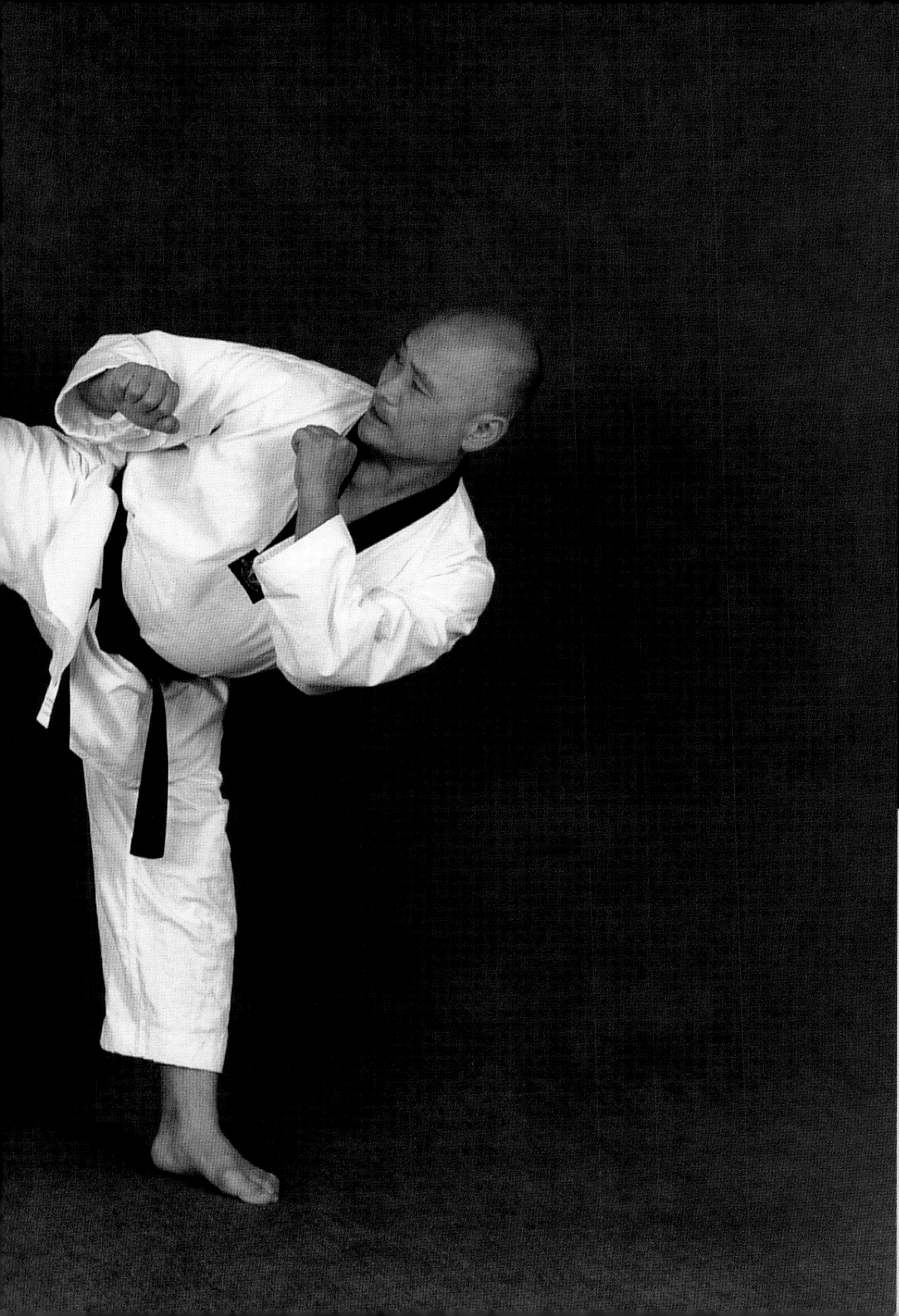

PART 2

BASIC ELEMENTS

Training Facilities

Martial arts are practiced in a specially designed facility or gym commonly called a *tojang* ("place of the way"). The practice area is designed to facilitate training while protecting trainees from injury. There should be no sharp corners or dangerous obstructions such as exposed columns or electrical wiring, glass cases, furniture, exposed hardware, or low ceilings and light fixtures. There should be adequate room to maneuver without running into walls or other people.

The flooring material used in Taekwondo schools varies widely and can be a range of materials including wood, tile, rubber, or carpeting. Whatever the surface, it must provide secure footing and be free of any surface aberrations that could lead to injuries. In some Taekwondo schools, the floor is covered with stiff padded mats that protect the trainee by absorbing and cushioning the body during falls. To avoid foot injuries from tripping, the mats must be placed flat without spaces between them. As tears develop, they must be promptly repaired or replaced. Over time, most mats shift from use, and should be periodically adjusted as required. Mirrors, punching bags, stretch bars, and various other devices are also used to assist training, and are frequently integrated into the training environment in various ways.

Uniform and Clothing

The jacket, belt, and pants worn during martial arts training is called a *tobok* ("clothing of the way") in Korean. The jacket and pants are normally white, and the belt (*tti* in Korean) is color-coded according to the student's rank. The belt is long enough to wrap twice around the waist and then tie in a square knot with two equal ends hanging loosely, 10 to 15 inches beyond the knot.

Martial arts uniforms are manufactured in a variety of fabric weights. Lighter weights are less restrictive of movement and usually more comfortable. Heavier weights resist tearing and usually last longer. Since grappling is usually not a part of Taekwondo training, and thus tearing not a concern, most practitioners prefer light-weight uniforms that wick away sweat and dry quickly.

Other garments often are worn under uniforms to enhance performance and protect the body. Mid-length or full-length tights are worn to support the muscles, retain heat, and wick sweat away from the body's surface. Many athletes also believe they help reduce muscle strains and pulls. Men should always wear appropriate groin support. Women should wear bras designed specifically for active sports. Leotards also are frequently worn for additional support and comfort.

Uniform Styles

Taekwondo uniforms are white. In many systems, black-belt practitioners are distinguished by black piping added in any number of locations, including the collar, edges of the jacket, cuffs, or along the length of the sleeve or pants. Currently, a wide variety of uniforms are being used by different schools. The most common is the modern V-neck top, with matching pants using an elastic waistband and drawstring. This style, which emerged in the 1970s, is widely favored for its comfort and functionality during a wide range of movements. However, it is inappropriate for grappling, since it tears easily. Many traditionally oriented styles continue to prefer the older style of jacket that is open and overlaps in the front. This style of jacket is more durable, but tends to open up and flap around during vigorous exercise, requiring the wearer to constantly stop and readjust their clothing.

Rank System

In most Korean, Japanese, and Okinawan martial arts, level of skill (rank) is designated by a colored belt worn around the waist. Before the twentieth century, most belts were colorless. Since students were prohibited from washing their belts, the belt grew progressively darker as a result of sweat and grime. When the colored belt system came into use, it was organized so that the belt color became progressively darker as the student advanced in rank. Most martial historians credit Jigoro Kano, Judo's founder, with being the originator of the color-belt ranking system.

Depending on the Taekwondo style you practice, there are 18 to 20 levels of rank, with 9 or 10 occurring before the black belt levels. The colored ranks below black belt are called grades (*kŭp* in Korean). The black ranks are referred to as degrees (*dan* in Korean). Black belt holders also have titles that denote rank. These titles vary based on the Taekwondo style one practices. Generally, black belt holders below 4th degree are called assistant instructors or instructors; black belt holders of 4th degree or higher are called masters or grandmasters, based on their rank. Some systems have attached philosophical meanings to the belt colors and the number of rank levels. However, this does not derive from any well known historical precedent, only a desire to somehow link the art to older philosophical traditions.

Ranks in Taekwondo are awarded based on skills and the amount of time spent in training at one's current rank. Promotion from one rank to another usually occurs through formal testing, which assesses a candidate's skills according to specific rank requirements. At the discretion of the instructor, ranks may also be awarded based primarily on training time. This is usually done for individuals who exhibit extreme dedication but possess physical limitations that make it impossible for them to perform certain techniques.

Taekwondo's ranking system, from lowest to highest rank, is given in the appendix. Note that belt color designations vary widely by school and federation, and have frequently been changed over time.

The specific skills required for each rank vary widely by school, style, and association. Generally, most tests involve skills demonstration, forms, sparring, breaking, and sometimes, a written essay and oral evaluation. In systems that focus on Olympic-Style competition, rank may also be awarded primarily based on success in competition. Skills testing usually ends at 5th or 6th degree, after which promotion is based on years of service and contributions to the art of Taekwondo. Ninth degrees are usually promoted by a federation and/or a consensus of 8th and 9th degrees. They are not self-appointed, or elected by their students. Historically, 10th degree was reserved for the founder or inheritor of a martial art style. This is not relevant in the case of Taekwondo.

Etiquette

Etiquette is the code of conduct and procedure by which you conduct yourself in the tojang. These traditional procedures are common to many martial arts and have been passed down through the centuries. Historically, many forms of etiquette arose for reasons of safety as well as respect. For example, the custom of shaking hands with one hand placed under the other, was done to show that you had no intention of drawing a weapon. The hands were plainly visible and signaled your peaceful intentions.

Bowing

Bowing, from either a standing or sitting position, is a sign of gratitude and respect found throughout the martial arts world. Westerners often misinterpret this as an act of submission, or see it as part of some deviant totalitarian ideal. This is incorrect. When you bow, it signifies not only respect for your instructors or superiors, but respect for yourself, the art, and "life" in general. It is a symbol of your profound regard and caring for the rights and lives of others. This reflects a basic attitude found throughout East Asian culture. For example, it is usually considered extremely bad form to embarrass or humiliate someone, even if they deserve it. If this happens, the offender is said to "lose face" and must correct the matter through some form of reparation and expression of humility toward the person offended. This form of behavior is quite foreign to many Westerners, for whom personal expression is sometimes placed before the feelings of others.

Bowing is normally done at the beginning and ending of practice sessions, sparring, and drills. You should also bow from the edge of the mat or practice area when entering and leaving, or when addressing an instructor.

Formal Sitting Bow

To perform a sitting bow, sit on both knees with your shins flush against the mat, knees shoulder width apart, hips resting on heels, hands on thighs. Bow by placing both palms on the mat in front of your knees, with the fingertips together and turned slightly inward. Bow from the waist as shown. A variation is sometimes used in which the toes and the balls of the feet are placed against the mat.

Informal Standing Bow

To perform a standing bow, place both heels together with toes angled outward. Place your open hands at your side, fingers together, shoulders pulled back. Bow from the waist. The command to bow in Korean is *Kyŏng-nye.*

Addressing Instructors

An instructor is always addressed as *sir* unless permission has been given to call him

Informal Bow from Standing Position

Formal Bow from Kneeling Position

or her by name. In Korean, there are different forms of "sir," depending upon the rank of the person addressed. An instructor is addressed as *sa-bŏm-nim,* a master as *kwan-jang-nim.* Never interrupt while an instructor is speaking, or another student is asking a question; give your full attention, remaining motionless. When an instructor finishes speaking, it is often customary to respond by saying *sir, sa-bom-nim,* or *kwan-jang-nim* to signify your understanding and enthusiasm.

School Etiquette

Every school has its own rules of etiquette. Some are very formal, others are quite relaxed. This is not a reflection of quality, but of choice. To assure that you do not cause any disrespect to your instructors, fellow students, or the school in general, always observe the following guidelines:

- Always address an instructor as "sir"
- Always bow when entering or leaving
- Never wear shoes on the mat
- Never wear unapproved or dirty uniforms
- Never sit or lie down unless directed
- Never spar unless directed
- Keep practicing until told to stop
- Never modify practice unless directed
- Always clean the practice area if asked
- Give instructors your full attention when they are speaking, remaining motionless

The Element of Risk

Martial arts can be a safe, rewarding, and physically beneficial practice. There is no reason to suffer debilitating injuries to enjoy its benefits or acquire its skills. However, you must be comfortable accepting the element of risk associated with the style you practice. Your age, health, conditioning, and athleticism all influence the level of risk. Before training and periodically thereafter, obtain a thorough medical examination. Be aware of limitations or existing physical conditions that may affect training. Advise your instructor, and never do *anything* in which you do not feel comfortable or safe. Remember, you are the best judge of your own limits, and the one who must live with the physical results of your actions.

Many forms of breathing and meditation are used in martial arts, to enhance physical performance, focus the mind, increase concentration, improve health, and cultivate spiritual sensitivity. Generally speaking, these techniques are not unique to Taekwondo or any other martial art, but come from the broader religious, philosophical, and medical, traditions common to many Eastern cultures. In Taekwondo, moving meditation and breath control are a fundamental part of training that impacts virtually all physical techniques.

MEDITATION

Meditation is a mental process characterized by contemplation or reflection. Throughout the world, there are many different forms of meditation, used for a variety of purposes. Meditation can lead a person to greater emotional stability and inner peace, positively affect physiological processes impacting health and well-being, and greatly increase one's ability to focus the mind. Meditation is also used to channel and control the circulation of Ki (internal energy) throughout the body, eventually allowing one to gain control of many body functions not normally controllable by conscious mental processes. Generally, most meditation techniques can be divided into two categories: stationary and moving. Stationary meditation is characterized by keeping the body relatively still. Moving meditation is characterized by physical movements. Many sophisticated meditation and energy-cultivation disciplines incorporate both stationary and moving techniques. Ki Gong is a typical example.

Taekwondo's Approach

Taekwondo is a martial art predicated on the development of speed, power, focused concentration, and the ability to make instantaneous correct actions in combat or in life. This requires a special form of concentration in which one is completely absorbed in the rapidly changing actions of the moment, but also aware of all that surrounds them. It is only natural that such a dynamic activity would mostly emphasize *moving* meditation practices, as opposed to *stationary* ones.

Generally, any form of physical exercise can become a form of moving meditation— jogging, swimming, rowing, etc. It is not the physical activity itself that is important, but rather one's mental actions during a chosen physical activity. In Taekwondo, the chosen activity is usually *forms*. The fundamental idea that forms are both a method of *combat training* and a form of *moving meditation* underlies virtually all systems of Taekwondo. While many forms have arguably become obsolete in terms of their combat value, their worth as moving meditation is timeless.

When first learning a new form, one is forced to concentrate on the mechanics of what one is doing. This strengthens various mental processes and focuses one's concentration, among other things. Eventually after much practice, the form becomes second nature; that is, one no longer consciously concentrates on correct motions or sequence. At this stage, the form's physical movements can become a platform for mental activities, similar to those explored and developed in stationary meditation—stilling the mind, focusing concentration, contemplation of emotional and spiritual matters, altering physiological processes, Ki cultivation, etc.

Taekwondo and Stationary Meditation

If one were to survey a range of Taekwondo systems, one would find there are many schools in which stationary meditation plays no role whatsoever; schools in which it is occasionally practiced; and schools in which it is an important integrated activity. The actual meditation techniques in use—as defined by specific postures, breathing and visualization methods, and physical actions—vary widely and are not consistent across Taekwondo as a whole. When stationary meditation is taught, techniques are invariably the reflection of a particular master's training and preferences, not some underlying system that is pervasive throughout Taekwondo. Consequently, this chapter will not be a recitation of any one particular form of stationary meditation, but a presentation of some of the basic ideas that underlie stationary meditation as a whole.

Meditation Principles

Virtually all forms of stationary meditation first begin with a conscious awareness of breath. It is this regulation of the mind and the breath that provides the foundation for further mental training.

Assume any comfortable posture. A few common postures are shown at lower-right, although many others are also used. Try to keep the spine elongated, with a slight natural curvature. Don't straighten it unnaturally or slouch. Clear your mind of emotional disturbances and try to become aware of your breath and the muscles that control it. Breathe slowly and deeply, down into the abdomen. Focus on being calm, continuous, and uniform, with an equal inhalation-exhalation cycle. The chest should remain mostly stationary. Inhale and exhale through your nose. There are various methods of timing the inhalation and exhalation cycle. In the beginning, just try to breathe with a natural rhythm. Gradually try to extend the length of your breathing cycle. For example: inhale for 8 seconds, exhale for 8 seconds.

As you breathe slowly and deeply, there are many different mental processes you can engage in, which are well defined in various meditation disciplines. One common method is to let your mind find its own focus, by not concentrating on any one particular thing. Be open to any awareness, but avoid becoming distracted, curious, analytical, or judgmental. Do not become consciously involved with whatever enters your mind; simply observe, thinking of nothing. Allow your awareness to become a reflection of your mind. If you have trouble maintaining concentration using this method or require something more concrete to focus on, try counting your breath cycles, observing your feelings, or focusing on physical sensations you feel in your body, internally or externally. For example, feelings of anger or joy, the touch of a gentle breeze caressing your face, the warmth of the sun on your back, the sound of the wind, the smell of rain, feelings in your organs or extremities, the flow of energy in your body, etc.

BREATH CONTROL

In Taekwondo, controlled breathing is used to maximize the body's performance, leading to increased speed, power, and endurance, and more focused concentration. Breath control is also used during strikes and blocks to help coordinate and time the body's actions, so power is focused at the moment of impact. Proper, well-timed breathing can also be used to increase the body's resistance to the effects of forceful blows to vital points.

Traditional Concepts

In traditionally oriented Taekwondo styles, breathing during the execution of a strike is characterized by momentarily holding the breath during delivery, then sharply exhaling at the moment of impact, as you tense the abdomen. This exhalation is very brief in duration and is usually accompanied by a loud shout, called a *Kihap*. This shout maximizes power and helps time the exhalation with the strike's impact. Your breathing during blocking techniques is usually characterized by a short, sharp exhalation, then momentarily holding the breath. This method of breath control not only powers the block, it is also used to fortify the blocker's body against blows to vital points (in case they are hit), in order to prevent loss of consciousness or recognition of pain. Slow inhalation is usually done between actions, in the pauses or calm spaces that typically occur during the flow of combat.

The Kihap-Shout

The distinct shout many martial artists emit when executing techniques is essentially breathing meditation converted to dynamic action. In Korean, this energy harmonizing shout is referred to as a *Kihap*. The word *Ki* is defined as the universal energy or dynamic force that animates all things. *Hap* is the root form for words which connote harmonizing, coming together, or coordinating. Thus the concept of *Kihap* literally means to harmonize with the dynamic universal life force. The "Kihap-shout" or "energy-harmonizing shout" is a means, then, of coordinating our actions with the flow of energies and events of which we are part. All individual actions and events merge into a single flow. This is what is meant by "being at one with the universe."

When you execute a punch or kick, or block a strike, energy is released—typically as a rush of air from the lungs. This exhalation of air, coordinated with muscular tension in the body and throat, creates the deep, roaring growl of the true Kihap-shout. When one first begins martial training, the shout is mostly an artificial decoration accompanying physical actions. However, if one focuses on the purpose of the shout, and practices in an uninhibited manner, one will eventually develop a shout that is a natural, spontaneous, uninhibited expression of the harmonized, total commitment of body, mind, and spirit to the techniques being executing.

Modern Concepts

In most high-intensity sports, performance is influenced by aerobic capacity (maximum amount of oxygen an athlete can utilize during continuous exercise). Around 80% of one's aerobic capacity is determined by genetics, the rest through training. Generally, athletes will exercise at a pulse rate that is 70% to 90% of their maximum heart rate (determined by genetics and age). This constitutes aerobic activity, meaning your muscles are driven by *aerobic* enzymes that require oxygen for metabolism. As long as your body supplies oxygen to the muscles, you can continue. As you increase exercise intensity, your body reaches a point when it no longer provides enough oxygen to maintain the metabolic demands of your muscles (called *anaerobic threshold*). At this point, your muscles continue to function by using *anaerobic* enzymes, which require no oxygen. These enzymes are used up after about two minutes, after which athletic performance declines dramatically.

Maximum aerobic fitness is achieved by vigorous exercising at least 5 days per week, and by including workouts that push you over your anaerobic threshold. One method is to rapidly alternate between high-intensity exercise that briefly elevates your pulse to its maximum level, and mild exercise that allows the pulse to drop to about 50% to 65% of maximum. Sustained high-intensity exercise also works, but produces more muscle pain.

Meditation Postures

Sitting with legs crossed, arms resting on thighs, hands closed or open

Kneeling with loose fists resting on thighs, insteps or balls of feet on floor

Kneeling with palms resting on thighs, insteps or balls of feet resting on floor

Standing relaxed with knees slightly bent, right hand over left, thumbs interlocked

How you stand and how you move are the basic building blocks of martial techniques. They are the key factors which make a specific technique, such as a punch or kick, possible. Different martial arts are often distinguished by preferences for certain types of foot and body positions, and certain methods of locomotion. Some styles prefer linear motions, some styles prefer circular motions, some blend the two together. In some arts, motions are free-flowing and continuous; in others they are abrupt, precise, and rigidly defined.

STANCES + MOVEMENT

In Taekwondo, stances are mostly designed to maximize power and speed during the execution of specific blocking and striking techniques. Historically, this involved stable, rooted stances and a preference for linear movement. Today the trend is toward greater mobility, and the seamless integration of stances with fast, fluid, sophisticated footwork, which can involve both linear and circular motions, particularly in Olympic-Style. The following pages show common stances and briefly discuss the basic forms of Taekwondo movement.

Overview

In any martial art, stances are defined by specific positions of the body and feet. These positions are normally used to execute specific techniques, or may become the linking points in a continuous movement. When body and feet relationships vary beyond certain defined limits, a "stance change" is said to have occurred. Generally speaking, it is better to think of stances as the links in a series of continuous movements, rather than as precisely defined foot placements. A rigid approach only limits your technique and your ability to adapt and improvise based on the constantly changing dynamics of combat.

Types of Stances

Taekwondo's stances are mostly designed to maximize power and speed during the execution of specific blocking and striking techniques. In most applications, the trunk is kept erect and the posture remains balanced. Some stances are offensive in nature; others are more suitable for defense. Some stances encourage, or are a part of, movement; others are stable. This chapter describes 28 stances commonly used in Taekwondo. They are organized into four basic categories:

- Natural Stances
- Fighting Stances
- Special Stances
- Olympic-Style Stances

Natural Stances

Natural stances resemble everyday standing postures, with the shoulders relaxed and the upper body erect. Historically, many of these postures were designed to prepare a person for a possible fight during a face-to-face confrontation, without signaling one's intent. Today, these stances are mostly used in formal settings occurring during the course of Taekwondo training or at demonstrations.

Fighting Stances

Fighting stances are specific postures in which the positions of the feet and body are optimized to facilitate execution of specific combative techniques, such as punches, kicks, blocks, and avoiding movements. There are many different types of Taekwondo fighting stances. Virtually all of them can be used to launch offensive or defensive actions, although most tend to be more suited to one or the other. For example, the Front Stance tends to be more offensive, whereas the Back Stance usually favors defense.

A variety of Taekwondo stances used during self-defense, sparring, or forms are shown on subsequent pages. Stances 16–20 are *transitional postures* that are usually a brief part of a continuous movement. Most stances in this chapter are demonstrated with the arms held downward and out to the sides, in order to emphasize the specific posture being depicted (foot placement, body position, balance). In actual self-defense or combat, the hands would either be held higher for protection, or involved in executing specific techniques. Practical applications showing stances in use are found throughout subsequent chapters.

Special Stances

Special stances are postures predominantly used in formal settings occurring during the course of Taekwondo training or at demonstrations or promotions. They are also used when practicing forms, or as preparatory postures leading to specific techniques.

Olympic-Style Stances

Olympic-Style stances are postures adapted from traditional Taekwondo stances, which were specially modified for use in Olympic-Style sport competition. In these stances, the position of the hands, feet, and body are optimized to facilitate quick execution of very specialized footwork and kicking techniques, the sole purpose of which is to score points and avoid being scored upon. The specific stances used tend to vary based on the style and preferences of individual competitors. Several stances currently in use are shown in this chapter. Please recognize that these postures are changing and evolving at a very rapid rate. These issues are further discussed in the author's 896-page Taekwondo book.

Stance Physics

S*tability* and *mobility* are important related concepts that define any stance. A stance's stability/mobility is largely determined by:

- The height of its center of gravity
- The area of its base
- The distribution of body weight

Center of gravity is largely determined by hip placement. Raising the hips (center of gravity) increases mobility and decreases stability. Conversely, lowering the hips increases stability and decreases mobility (example 1).

The *base area* of a stance is determined by foot placement. Moving the feet closer together increases mobility but decreases stability. Moving the feet farther apart has the opposite effect (example 2).

The *distribution of body weight* is determined by lateral placement of the hips and torso, which translates into a percentage of total weight over each foot (e.g., 70% rear foot, 30% front foot). This influences directional stability and mobility, depending on which foot is weighted and by how much (example 3).

In actual fighting, center of gravity, base area, and weight distribution are always in a state of flux—the hips rise, fall, and shift laterally; the feet move closer and farther apart; body weighting constantly shifts between feet. Mobility and stability are constantly changing based on the demands of technique.

Hand Positions

The formation of the hands and arms can be varied in many ways, depending on tactics and techniques. The specific position you adopt is called a "guard." Typical guards are shown at right and throughout this chapter; however, they are not the only acceptable ones. Generally, your hand position should provide defense, while facilitating speed and power. In Taekwondo, the hands are usually formed in fists that are untensed, until punches or blocks are applied. This keeps you relaxed, promoting speed and fluidity.

Types of Stances

Natural Stance

Fighting Stance

Special Stance

Olympic-Style Stance

Stance Stability vs Mobility

1. *Changes in center of gravity height*

2. *Changes in base area*

3. *Changes in weight distribution*

Stance Relationships

Open stance and *closed stance* are terms that define how an opponent's targets are placed relative to you, which influences tactics and techniques. In an open stance, frontal targets of the body appear open to the opponent. This occurs when one person leads with the left side and the other leads with the right. In a closed stance, frontal targets of the body appear closed to the opponent. This occurs when both persons lead with the same side (e.g., right leads). Examples are shown at right. Understanding how stance relationships relate to specific skills is important when analyzing an opponent's tactics and probable range of techniques. This relationship also influences your own choices.

Open Stances

Closed Stances

STANCE SUMMARY

Stance		Balance	Comments
	Natural Stances		
1	Attention Stance	Equal	Used in formal settings or to prepare for an action.
2	Close Stance	Equal	Used in formal settings or to prepare for an action.
3	Parallel Stance	Equal	Basic ready stance used to prepare for an action; feet are parallel.
4	Outward Stance	Equal	Same as stance 3, except feet turned outward.
5	Inward Stance	Equal	Same as stance 3, except feet turned inward. Rarely used except as exercise.
	Fighting Stances		
6	Riding Stance	Equal	Face forward or sideways; often used to practice punching fundamentals.
7	Inward Riding Stance	Equal	Face forward or sideways; used to make sudden stops or changes of direction.
8	Diagonal Stance	Equal	Face forward or sideways; more stable than stance 6; easy to pivot to other stances.
9	Inward Diagonal Stance	Equal	Face forward or sideways. Used to make sudden stops or changes of direction.
10	Walking Stance	Equal	Versatile stance; often used for attacking to the front or rear.
11	Low Walking Stance	Equal	Used to generate quick, explosive motions in a forward direction.
12	Front Stance	Equal	Powerful stance for forward attacks; good stability, low mobility.
13	Back Stance	70% rear foot	Basic defensive stance; favors backward footwork and front-leg kicks.
14	T Stance	70% rear foot	Similar to stance 13, but groin more protected; facilitates turning counterkicks.
15	Tiger Stance	90–100% rear foot	Flexible stance; good mobility, poor stability; favors use of front-leg.
16	Assisting Stance	90–100% front foot	Transitional posture used to launch a quick forward action or stop suddenly.
17	Front Cross Stance	90% one foot	Transitional posture used during lateral movement.
18	Back Cross Stance	90% one foot	Transitional posture used during lateral or forward movement.
19	Crane Stance	One-leg raised	Transitional posture used to launch kicks, or as a balance-strengthening exercise
20	Reverse Crane Stance	One-leg raised	Transitional posture used to launch Back Kicks, or stabilize balance when thrusting.
	Special Stances		
21	Basic Ready Stance	Equal	Used in formal settings, to prepare for an action, or at the completion of an action.
22	Fist-Waist Ready Stance	Equal	Used in formal settings or to prepare for an action.
23	Lapped-Hands Ready Stance	Equal	Used in formal settings or to prepare for an action.
24	Covered-Fist Ready Stance	Equal	Used in formal settings or to prepare for an action; mostly used in forms.
25	Push-Hands Ready Stance	Equal	Used in formal settings or to prepare for an action; mostly used in forms.
	Olympic-Style Stances		
26	45° Fighting Stance	Equal, shifting	Basic fighting stance; suitable for most techniques.
27	Side Fighting Stance	Equal, shifting	Basic fighting stance; useful for launching Side Kicks or Back Kicks.
28	Low Fighting Stance	Equal, shifting	Low stance; useful for countering with Roundhouse Kicks or turning kicks.

Twenty-eight common Taekwondo stances are summarized at left and shown below. These stances are shown in greater detail in the author's 896-page Taekwondo book.

1. Attention

2. Close Stance

3. Parallel Stance

4. Outward Stance

5. Inward Stance

6. Riding Stance

7. Inward Riding Stance

8. Diagonal Stance

9. Inward Diagonal Stance

10. Walking Stance

11. Low Walking Stance

12. Front Stance

13. Back Stance

14. T Stance

15. Tiger Stance

16. Assisting Stance

17. Front Cross Stance

18. Back Cross Stance

19. Crane Stance

20. Reverse Crane Stance

21. Basic Ready Stance

22. Fist-Waist Ready

23. Lapped-Hands Ready

24. Covered-Fist Ready

25. Push-Hands Ready

26. 45° Fighting Stance

27. Side Fighting Stance

28. Low Fighting Stance

Overview

In the martial arts there are many forms of movement, such as stepping, hopping, jumping, knee-walking, tumbling, rolling, and crawling. Taekwondo predominantly focuses on stand-up fighting; therefore, footwork is vitally important. In contrast, eclectic arts, such as Hapkido, encompass both stand-up and ground fighting; so for them, standing and ground movement are equally important. In Taekwondo, like most martial arts, the purpose of movement is to optimize your body's placement with respect to your opponent's. Specific movements are used to facilitate execution of offensive or defensive technique, or to remove oneself from harm's way. All forms of Taekwondo movement possess the same objectives:

• Avoid an attack
• Launch an attack or counterattack
• Maximize the efficiency of techniques
• Disrupt the opponent's tactics
• Create an opening in opponent's defense
• Create flaws in opponent's movements
• Preserve a standing posture
• Avoid ground fighting

Footwork Principles

The key element in standing movement is footwork, although hip and torso motions also play crucial supporting roles. The placement of the feet (stance) influences mobility, speed, power, balance, and the range of usable techniques. Superior footwork can often offset disadvantages in size, strength, and degree of skill—particularly important when facing larger opponents. Footwork changes according to your tactics, which are influenced by: an opponent's stance, position, distance, and tactics; the number of opponents; and footing conditions (e.g., slippery, stable). Good footwork is characterized by:

• Moving the body fluidly, staying relaxed
• Coordinating the entire body as one unit
• Moving lightly on the balls of the feet
• Making purposeful movements
• Maintaining balance throughout movement
• Modifying stances to maximize technique

Body Movement

Footwork is always integrated with overall body movement. The use of the hips and shoulders is important for generating movement (particularly spins) and setting up the use of the feet or hands for striking or blocking. Rotation of the torso and hips is also used to increase the efficiency of punches and kicks. In summary, hip, shoulder, and head movements are used to:

• Generate directional movement
• Generate power
• Shift balance
• Feint or distract
• Maximize the efficiency of techniques

Types of Footwork

Almost all footwork in Taekwondo derives from about 37 basic stepping methods, which are combined or altered to create innumerable possibilities. In the author's Taekwondo books, basic steps are classified as follows:

• Forward Footwork
• Backward Footwork
• Lateral Footwork
• Turning Footwork
• Drawing Footwork
• Crossing Footwork
• Shifting Footwork

The 37 basic steps are shown on the following pages. The numbers in the text below, and list at far right, correspond to the illustrations found on subsequent pages. Photos, further explanation, combination steps, and practical applications are shown in the author's 896-page Taekwondo book.

1–3 Forward Footwork

Forward footwork is usually used to move closer to an attacker, in order to secure a better attacking position, launch a strike, hinder an opponent's ability to launch kicks, or retreat from an opponent behind you. There are three types of forward footwork: Forward Step, Forward Slide, and Forward Shuffle. In a *Forward Step,* the rear foot steps forward (past the front foot) and the front foot pivots. In a *Forward Slide* and *Forward Shuffle,* both feet slide forward maintaining the same stance. In a slide, the rear foot moves first. In a shuffle, the front foot moves first.

4–6 Backward Footwork

Backward footwork is usually used to move away from an attacker, in order to avoid an attack, make room for a kick, secure a better position, or advance toward an opponent behind you. There are three types of backward footwork: Back Step, Back Slide, and Back Shuffle. All backward footwork is the opposite of forward footwork which bears the same name. For instance, a Forward Step executed in reverse sequence is a Back Step.

7–16 Lateral Footwork

Lateral footwork is used to move sideways for the same tactical reasons outlined under forward and backward footwork. Although there are 10 basic lateral steps, in practical use these steps are varied in innumerable ways depending upon tactics and technique. Variables include step angle and direction, step sequence, length of step, foot placement, forward or backward movement, degree of body rotation, planted or sliding pivot-foot, and stances selected. Lateral footwork is far more complex and varied than forward or backward footwork, and is an important element in any martial artist's technique. It is frequently ignored, but is essential for quick countering, operating in restricted spaces, or penetrating the defenses of skilled opponents.

There are three types of lateral footwork: Side Step, Side Slide, and Side Slide–Step. In a *Side Step,* one foot steps 45° to 90° sideways while the other foot pivots. There are four side-step variations, depending upon which direction you step (left or right) and which foot pivots. In a *Side Slide,* both feet slide sideways, maintaining the same stance. There are four variations, depending on which direction you step and which foot pivots. In a *Side Slide–Step,* the rear foot steps sideways-forward and the front foot steps 45° to 90° sideways. There are two variations, depending on which direction you step (left or right).

17–22 Turning Footwork

There are three basic types of turning movement: Turn Step, Pivot, and Step-Pivot. In a *Turn Step* the body rotates 180° toward the rear side, while moving forward. Turn Steps are typically used to launch a Back Fist, Back Kick, Whip Kick, or Hook Kick, or to turn and face an opponent behind you while moving away. In a *Pivot,* both feet pivot to face an opponent coming in from the side or from behind; there is no step. From a Back Stance you may pivot 180°, from a Front Stance about 135°. To increase a Front Stance pivot to 180° of rotation, a *Step-Pivot* is used. In this movement, one foot steps sideways, then both feet pivot to face an opponent coming from the side or behind. The *Pivot* and the *Step-Pivot* are also used to alternate between multiple opponents.

23–26 Drawing Footwork

In drawing footwork one foot is drawn along the ground toward the other, while the opposite foot kicks, blocks, or steps toward the original position of the drawing foot. The Draw Step is usually used to *quickly* launch leg blocks or kicks while moving forward or backwards. It is often used in countering kicks or to create an opening for subsequent techniques. In Draw Steps, kicks are launched much more quickly than with traditional stance changes. A Draw Step can also be used to assume the opposite stance while maintaining the same position (front foot becomes rear foot, rear becomes front). In Draw Steps, separate foot movements should appear to be almost simultaneous. Draw Steps are easily modified into advancing or retreating versions that integrate forward and backward footwork.

27–30 Crossing Footwork

In Cross Steps, one foot crosses over the other while stepping forward or backward. A Cross Step is often used to close distance when kicking. Because one foot crosses over the other it is possible to cover a greater distance than a Forward Step would allow. However, if your opponent catches you while you step, you are very vulnerable to being knocked off-balance or thrown. There are four Cross Step variations, which set up different directions of hip rotation. The step used is based on the technique to be executed. A *Cross Step Behind* is usually more appropriate for executing outside strikes such as the Hook Kick, Outside Crescent Kick, or Back Fist. A *Cross Step Front* is considered more appropriate for executing inside kicks such as the Roundhouse Kick or Inside Crescent Kick. A Side Kick can be executed using either step, although the *behind* version is usually preferred, as it frees up the kicking leg. A *Cross Step Behind–Pivot* or a *Cross Step Front–Pivot* is used to keep turning when addressing multiple opponents in restricted spaces. Cross Steps can be executed moving forward or backward from any stance. The Side Stance is most common, since it more efficiently positions the feet for stepping.

31–37 Shifting Footwork

There are five types of shifting footwork. A *Spot Shift* is a short, quick, hopping motion in which both feet shift their position simultaneously. A *One-Foot Shift* is a short movement in which one foot shifts it position while the other remains stationary or pivots slightly. *Jumping* is a form of movement in which both feet are airborne during the step. A *Pivot Shift* and a *Toe Shift* are very short, deceptive motions in which both feet slide simultaneously, usually to creep closer.

Footwork Diagrams

The footwork drawings on the following pages illustrate foot placement for the basic steps previously outlined. In actual use the placement of the feet varies depending upon a variety of tactical factors. For example, when executing a Back Slide, the rear foot might be placed anywhere within a 45° arc depending on circumstances. When a Back Step no longer is a Back Step, but a Side Step, is of academic concern only. The specific stances shown in the drawings are for purposes of illustration only. These basic steps can be executed from a variety of stances, each of which will possess specific advantages or limitations.

Types of Footwork

Forward Footwork
1 Forward Step
2 Forward Slide
3 Forward Shuffle

Backward Footwork
4 Back Step
5 Back Slide
6 Back Shuffle

Lateral Footwork
7 Side Step–Front Pivot (left)
8 Side Step–Front Pivot (right)
9 Side Step–Back Pivot (left)
10 Side Step–Back Pivot (right)
11 Side Slide (front left)
12 Side Slide (front right)
13 Side Slide (back left)
14 Side Slide (back right)
15 Side Slide–Step (left)
16 Side Slide–Step (right)

Turning Footwork
17 Turn Step (face forward)
18 Turn Step (face behind)
19 Pivot (face side)
20 Pivot (face behind)
21 Step-Pivot (front step)
22 Step-Pivot (back step)

Drawing Footwork
23 Front Draw
24 Front Draw Turning
25 Rear Draw
26 Rear Draw Turning

Crossing Footwork
27 Cross Step Behind
28 Cross Step Front
29 Cross Step Behind–Pivot
30 Cross Step Front–Pivot

Shifting Footwork
31 Spot Shift (forward)
32 Spot Shift (backward)
33 Spot Shift (diagonally)
34 One-Foot Shift
35 Pivot Shift
36 Jumping
37 Toe Shift

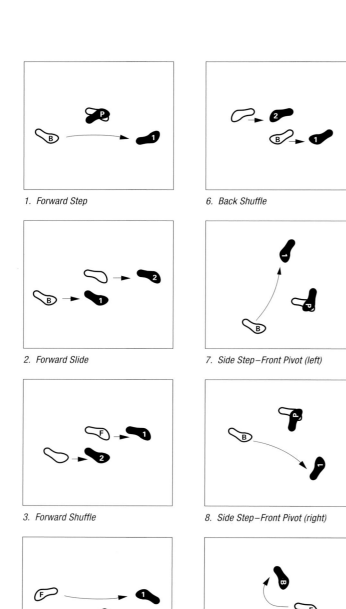
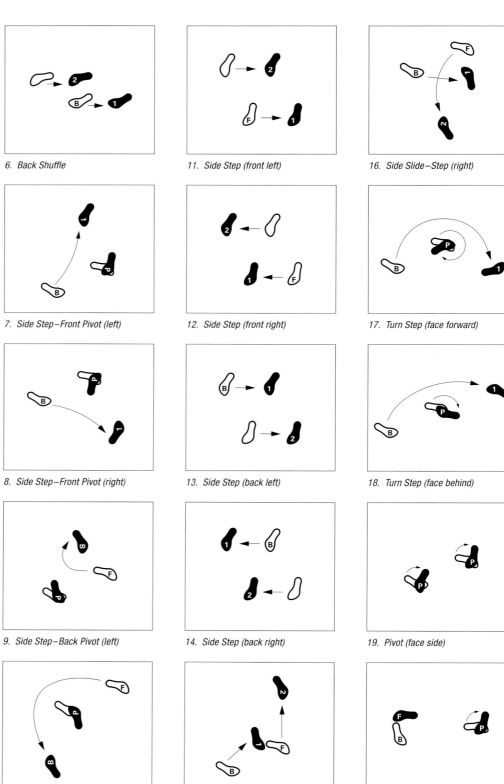

1. Forward Step

2. Forward Slide

3. Forward Shuffle

4. Back Step

5. Back Slide

6. Back Shuffle

7. Side Step–Front Pivot (left)

8. Side Step–Front Pivot (right)

9. Side Step–Back Pivot (left)

10. Side Step–Back Pivot (right)

11. Side Step (front left)

12. Side Step (front right)

13. Side Step (back left)

14. Side Step (back right)

15. Side Slide–Step (left)

16. Side Slide–Step (right)

17. Turn Step (face forward)

18. Turn Step (face behind)

19. Pivot (face side)

20. Pivot (face behind)

Almost all standing footwork in Taekwondo derives from about 37 basic steps, which are combined or altered to create innumerable possibilities. Photos, further explanation, and practical applications are found in the author's 896-page Taekwondo book.

Outlined feet indicate start position; *solid* feet indicate ending. Numbers indicate which foot moves first.

P	Pivot
B	Back Foot
F	Front Foot
1, 2	Sequence

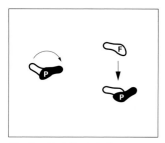

21. Step-Pivot (front step)

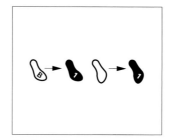

26. Rear Draw Turning

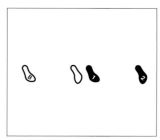

31. Spot Shift (forward)

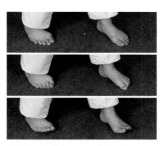

36. Jumping (see note below)

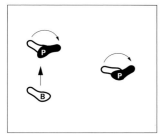

22. Step-Pivot (back step)

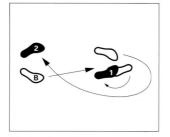

27. Cross Step Behind

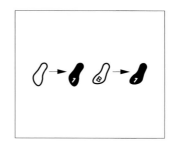

32. Spot Shift (backward)

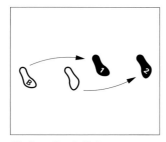

37. Toe Shift (see note below)

Note:

36: Jumping steps can be straight up or in any direction. Jumps are often based on the basic steps covered previously. The drawing shows a jump based on a Forward Slide (2), which is often used to launch lead kicks.

37: A Toe Shift is used to sneak closer to an opponent undetected.
Pull your feet forward by repeatedly gripping and pulling the floor with your toes, shifting 1 to 2 inches per pull.

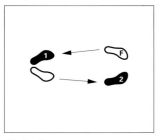

23. Front Draw

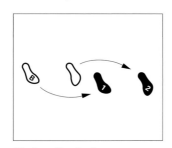

28. Cross Step Front

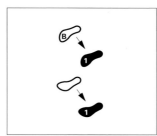

33. Spot Shift (diagonally)

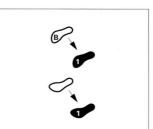

24. Front Draw Turning

29. Cross Step Behind–Pivot

34. One-Foot Shift

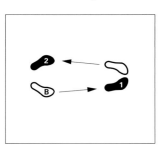

25. Rear Draw

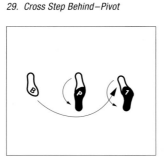

30. Cross Step Front–Pivot

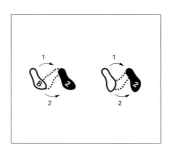

35. Pivot Shift

Attack points are the specific parts of your body (hands, feet, elbows, forearms, knees, etc.) which are used to attack specific targets and execute specific techniques. The method of attack is usually a strike; however, these same body surfaces are often used when applying blocks. The use of a particular attack point usually involves specific formations of the hand or foot. Historically, Taekwondo used about thirty-eight attack points, although in recent decades the trend is toward greater simplicity by using fewer points.

ATTACK POINTS + TARGETS

Taekwondo training also includes the study of human anatomy. Detailed knowledge of vital targets is used to magnify the effect of strikes or blocks, or to protect one's vulnerable areas. The illustrations on subsequent pages show the anatomical targets commonly used in Taekwondo, the three most basic being the philtrum (upper lip), solar plexus, and groin. Readers seeking an in-depth overview of Western and Eastern concepts of the human body should obtain the author's book "Essential Anatomy For Healing and Martial Arts."

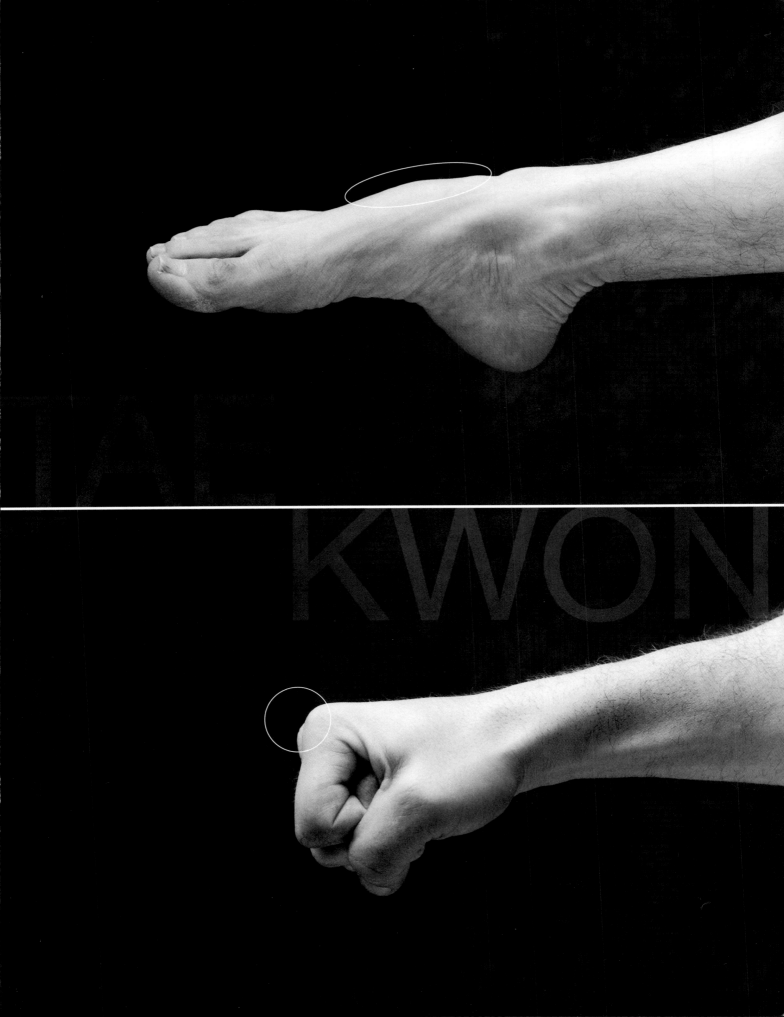

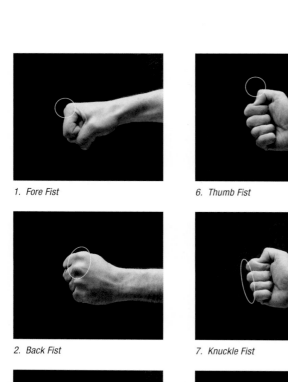

1. Fore Fist

6. Thumb Fist

11. Back Hand

16. Three-Finger Spear Hand

2. Back Fist

7. Knuckle Fist

12. Flat Spear Hand

17. Angle Spear Hand

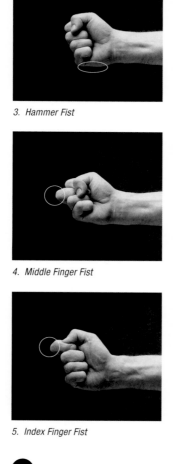

3. Hammer Fist

8. Flat Fist

13. Two-Finger Spear Hand

18. Fingertip Hand

4. Middle Finger Fist

9. Knife Hand

14. Scissor Spear Hand

19A. Palm Heel Hand (option 1)

5. Index Finger Fist

10. Ridge Hand

15. One-Finger Spear Hand

19B. Palm Heel Hand (option 2)

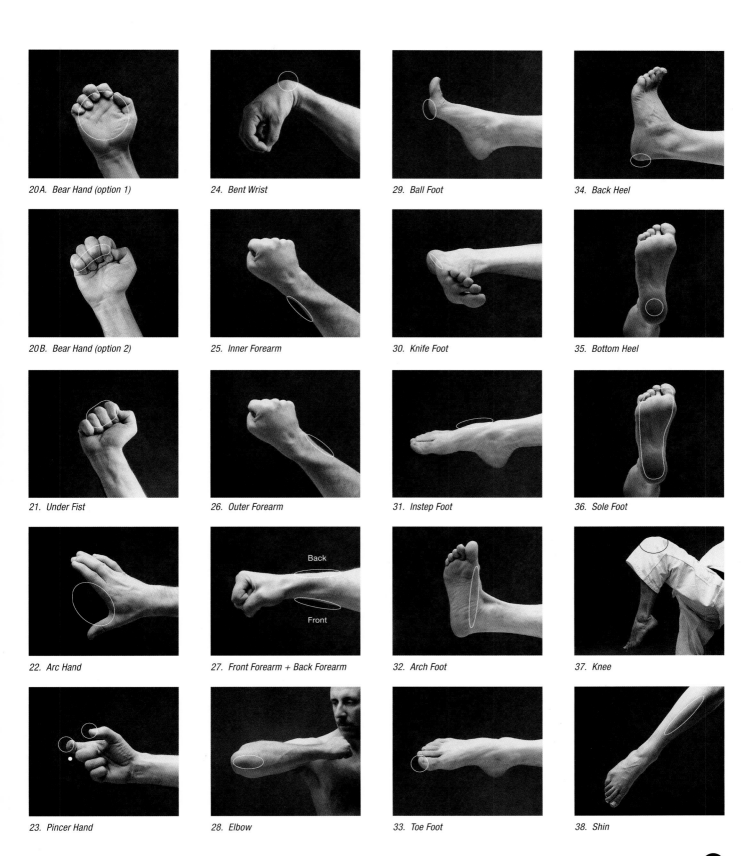

20A. Bear Hand (option 1)

24. Bent Wrist

29. Ball Foot

34. Back Heel

20B. Bear Hand (option 2)

25. Inner Forearm

30. Knife Foot

35. Bottom Heel

21. Under Fist

26. Outer Forearm

31. Instep Foot

36. Sole Foot

22. Arc Hand

27. Front Forearm + Back Forearm

Back

Front

32. Arch Foot

37. Knee

23. Pincer Hand

28. Elbow

33. Toe Foot

38. Shin

The following drawings identify vital targets using basic Western medical terminology. Damage to these anatomically weak points can cause trauma to blood vessels, nerves, bones, tissue, and joints—either separately or in unison. For example, striking the temple may cause a concussion, a skull fracture, neck trauma (whiplash), damage to cranial nerves, arteries, and veins; all of the above; or none of the above (the strike could be ineffective). The level of damage depends on force, angle of attack, method of attack (strike, press, hold), hitting surface (fist, weapon), and individual anatomy (bone mass, musculature, etc.).

Head Area

The head, face, and lower edge of the jaw contain numerous *cranial nerves,* well exposed to strikes or pressing holds. Head blows may cause a concussion by slamming the brain against the skull cavity (usually 180° opposite of the blow). This causes bleeding into the brain and death of brain cells, resulting in dizziness, confusion, loss of consciousness, or even death. Blows to the chin are usually directed sideways, causing the TMJ (joint) to fracture at the back of the mandible, especially when the jaw is open. The nose is structurally weakest when struck from the side, although a frontal blow is also painful. Eye strikes can result in corneal abrasion, globe rupture, retinal detachment, or fracture of the socket surrounding the eye.

Neck Area

Major blood vessels (carotid, jugular) and nerves (cervical, supraclavicular, auricular, vagus, accessory) are all concentrated close to the sternocleidomastoid muscle, at the side of the neck. Chokes applied at this point restrict blood flow to the brain, resulting in loss of consciousness or death. Blows to the back or side of the neck can dislocate cervical vertebrae or damage nerve roots, impairing motor functions. Accessory nerve damage paralyzes sternocleidomastoid and trapezius muscles, resulting in an inability to raise the shoulder or turn the head. Violently twisting the head can fracture vertebrae, causing paralysis or death. A blow to the larynx, trachea, or surrounding cartilage can cause obstruction of the airway and bleeding into the throat—injuries which can be fatal.

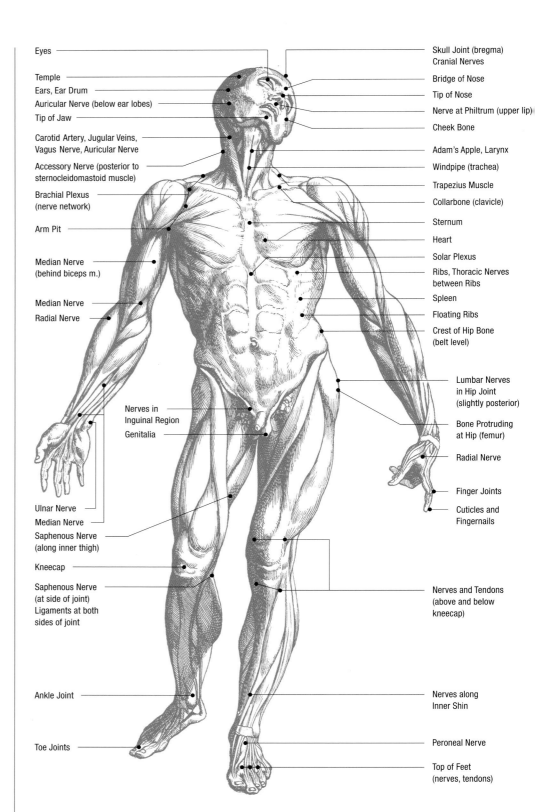

Eyes

Temple

Ears, Ear Drum

Auricular Nerve (below ear lobes)

Tip of Jaw

Carotid Artery, Jugular Veins, Vagus Nerve, Auricular Nerve

Accessory Nerve (posterior to sternocleidomastoid muscle)

Brachial Plexus (nerve network)

Arm Pit

Median Nerve (behind biceps m.)

Median Nerve
Radial Nerve

Nerves in Inguinal Region
Genitalia

Ulnar Nerve
Median Nerve
Saphenous Nerve (along inner thigh)

Kneecap

Saphenous Nerve (at side of joint)
Ligaments at both sides of joint

Ankle Joint

Toe Joints

Skull Joint (bregma)
Cranial Nerves

Bridge of Nose

Tip of Nose

Nerve at Philtrum (upper lip)

Cheek Bone

Adam's Apple, Larynx

Windpipe (trachea)

Trapezius Muscle

Collarbone (clavicle)

Sternum

Heart

Solar Plexus

Ribs, Thoracic Nerves between Ribs

Spleen

Floating Ribs

Crest of Hip Bone (belt level)

Lumbar Nerves in Hip Joint (slightly posterior)

Bone Protruding at Hip (femur)

Radial Nerve

Finger Joints

Cuticles and Fingernails

Nerves and Tendons (above and below kneecap)

Nerves along Inner Shin

Peroneal Nerve

Top of Feet (nerves, tendons)

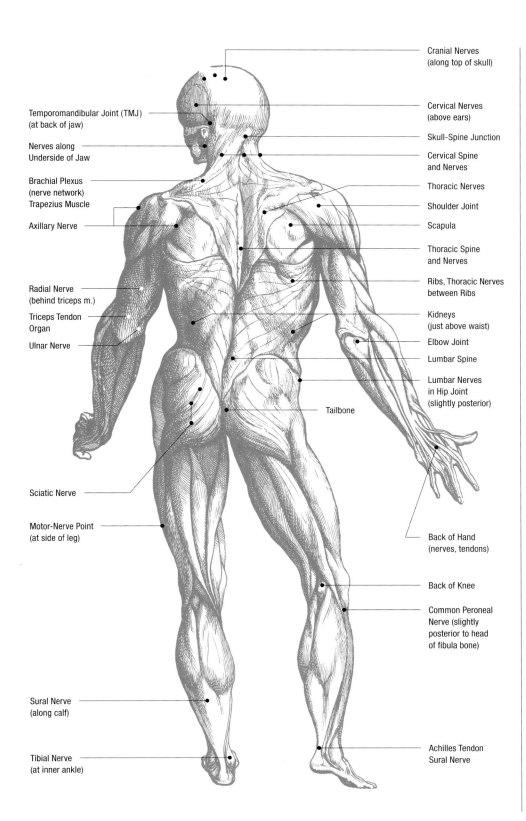

Cranial Nerves
(along top of skull)

Temporomandibular Joint (TMJ)
(at back of jaw)

Nerves along
Underside of Jaw

Brachial Plexus
(nerve network)
Trapezius Muscle

Axillary Nerve

Cervical Nerves
(above ears)

Skull-Spine Junction

Cervical Spine
and Nerves

Thoracic Nerves

Shoulder Joint

Scapula

Radial Nerve
(behind triceps m.)

Triceps Tendon
Organ

Ulnar Nerve

Thoracic Spine
and Nerves

Ribs, Thoracic Nerves
between Ribs

Kidneys
(just above waist)

Elbow Joint

Lumbar Spine

Lumbar Nerves
in Hip Joint
(slightly posterior)

Tailbone

Sciatic Nerve

Motor-Nerve Point
(at side of leg)

Back of Hand
(nerves, tendons)

Back of Knee

Common Peroneal
Nerve (slightly
posterior to head
of fibula bone)

Sural Nerve
(along calf)

Tibial Nerve
(at inner ankle)

Achilles Tendon
Sural Nerve

Shoulder Area

The *brachial plexus* is a network of cervical and thoracic nerves (median, radial, ulnar, axillary, musculocutaneous) which form the entire nerve supply for the upper extremities and shoulder area. The nerves lie close together as they pass from the top of the shoulder, behind the collarbone, along the front of the joint, and down to the armpit, where they branch into the arm. They are very vulnerable to blows or pressure directed to the areas indicated. The collarbone is easily fractured or separated by a direct blow or fall. Joint-lock holds or a throw can dislocate the shoulder. Blows to the back of the shoulder or scapula can damage a variety of thoracic nerves (especially if near the spine).

Trunk Area

The *solar plexus* is a nerve network found below the sternum. Blows to the solar plexus hinder breathing by causing transient paralysis of the diaphragm (see note, next page). Blows to the sternum can cause trauma to the heart. Ribs are easily fractured by forceful blows (especially floating ribs) and may puncture the lungs or other organs. Lateral or posterior blows can rupture the spleen, while posterior blows to the kidneys can cause bruising or severe internal bleeding. Strikes to the genitalia are painful, but not always debilitating. Strikes to the spinal column can damage nerves, resulting in transient or permanent paralysis.

Arm and Leg Areas

The elbow, wrist, and finger joints are frequently attacked with twisting or breaking holds due to their inherent weakness and susceptibility to pain. Nerve attacks to hands, fingernails, and elbows are usually used to release a hold, distract, or assist applying a hold. The knee is probably the most vulnerable target on the legs. It is structurally quite weak and can be attacked from any direction. If you damage your opponent's knee(s), you normally take away that person's ability to maneuver or continue the fight. The kneecap almost always dislocates laterally, so horizontal or 45° angular blows are most efficient. Strikes or pressing attacks to leg nerves will usually weaken the leg or cause a fall. Small fragile foot bones are easily damaged or broken by being stomped on.

In the martial arts as a whole, there are many different approaches to striking, ranging from soft styles that use light to moderate force to hit precise pressure points, to hard styles that direct significant force to larger vulnerable areas. In Taekwondo, the focus is primarily on developing powerful penetrating strikes, delivered with strengthened and hardened body surfaces to parts of the body that are structurally weak. The objective is frequently to break bone or damage organs and tissue by striking vital or vulnerable areas. In contrast,

STRIKES + BLOCKS

blocking techniques are usually executed with less force, although a powerful, well-timed block to an appropriate target can easily damage an opponent's limbs, hindering their ability or desire to continue. While many of the motions employed in Taekwondo's strikes and blocks appear simple and easy to learn, they can take a long time to truly understand and perfect. Time, patience, and constant repetition is the foundation of Taekwondo training, and the only way to true mastery. The following pages provide a brief overview of basic skills.

The ten strikes and five blocks shown in this chapter demonstrate basic motions used in many Taekwondo striking and blocking techniques. Some of these examples are among the first techniques novice students will learn. Many masters feel that perfecting these skills lays a foundation upon which further techniques are more easily learned. These photos are not intended to be instructional, but rather to give the reader a general sense of the stances, motions, and unique qualities that define Taekwondo strike and blocks; many other motions are also used. Be aware that kicks used in Olympic-Style sparring are sometimes applied using slightly different deliveries or attack points. A brief overview of Taekwondo's striking and blocking techniques was previously given in Part 1 of this book, under *Technique Overview*. For further information, please reference the author's 896-page Taekwondo book, which contains detailed photos and descriptions of more than 180 basic strikes and blocks, including skills widely used in Olympic-Style sparring.

1. Straight Punch

The Fore Fist follows a straight path and is rotated 90° to 180°, as your other fist retracts to your hip. A *Lunge Punch* is a lead-hand blow; a *Reverse Punch* is a rear-hand blow.

2. Inside Knife Hand Strike

The Knife Hand follows an inward, circular horizontal path. The hand rotates at least 180°, as your other fist retracts to your hip.

3. Outside Knife Hand Strike

The Knife Hand follows an outward, circular horizontal path. The hand rotates about 90° as your other fist retracts to your hip.

4. Hook Punch

The Fore Fist follows a short, horizontal circular path, with the elbow bent about 90°. The punching fist rotates 90° to 180°, as your opposite fist retracts to your hip.

5. Rising Elbow Strike

The elbow thrusts forward and up in a vertical arc, as you retract your other fist to your hip.

1. Straight Punch

2. Inside Knife Hand Strike

3. Outside Knife Hand Strike

4. Hook Punch

5. Rising Elbow Strike

6. Front Kick

The Ball Foot follows an upward vertical circular path with the chambered knee initially pointing toward the target, as the lower leg snaps forward. The support leg is slightly flexed with the foot planted.

7. Side Kick

The leg is raised with the knee fully bent. The Knife Foot is thrust straight forward as the hips turn over and the supporting leg pivots 180° (support heel points to the target). The foot is retracted along the same path. You can also strike with the Bottom Heel.

Back Kick

This kick is mechanically similar to the Side Kick, except it is directed either: to your rear; or to an opponent in front, when preceded by a Turn Step (see *Stances + Movement* chapter). The kicking knee typically brushes the supporting knee as it passes backward. The Bottom Heel is used for hitting. Different types of Back Kicks, including Olympic-Style versions, are covered in the author's 896-page Taekwondo book. In this book, examples of Turning Back Kicks are found in *Part 4: Olympic-Style Sparring*.

8. Roundhouse Kick

The leg is raised with the knee pointing directly at the target. The lower leg snaps forward in a horizontal arc, as the support leg pivots 180°. This kick is commonly applied with the Instep Foot or Ball Foot.

9. Hook Kick

The leg is raised with the knee bent. Rotate the kicking hip forward and thrust your foot forward and slightly to the outside of the target. As your leg reaches full extension, suddenly snap your Back Heel toward the target by rapidly bending your knee, keeping your kicking thigh stationary.

10. Downward Kick

Swing the foot up high, with the knee extended, then slam your foot down into the target, thrusting your hips forward for power. Hit with the Back Heel, Ball Foot, or Sole Foot.

6. Front Kick

7. Side Kick

8. Roundhouse Kick

9. Hook Kick

10. Downward Kick

1. Rising Block

This block is used to deflect high straight strikes, circular strikes, or descending strikes directed to the head (high section). Block upward, from underneath the blow, using a rising motion as you twist the Outer Forearm into the attacker's arm or leg. Your forearm should finish at an angle, with the arm slightly above and in front of the head. As you block, pull your other hand to your hip.

2. Low Block

This block is used to deflect low straight strikes to the lower abdomen or groin, such as a Front Kick. The twisting forearm follows an outward and downward path across your body and deflects the strike to the side, using the Outer Forearm. Finish with the palm facing downward. Pull your other hand to your hip.

3. Inside Block

This block is used to deflect straight or circular strikes directed at the head or middle section. The forearm follows an *inward* path across your body and deflects the strike to the side, as you twist your Outer Forearm into the attacker's arm or leg. The forearm finishes vertical or at a slightly forward angle, bent 90° at the elbow. Pull your other hand to your hip.

4. Outside Block

This block is used to deflect straight or circular strikes directed at the head or middle section. The forearm follows an *outward* path across your body and deflects the blow to the side, as you twist the Inner Forearm into the attacker's arm or leg. Finish with the palm facing toward you. The forearm finishes at a forward angle, and is bent about 90° at the elbow. Pull your other hand to your hip.

5. Outside Knife Block

This block uses the Knife Hand to deflect strikes directed to the head or middle section. The hand follows an outward path and deflects the strike to the side using the edge of the hand. Finish with your blocking palm facing forward, elbow aligned with your body, bent about 90°. The assisting Knife Hand finishes with the palm facing upward.

1. Rising Block

2. Low Block

3. Inside Block

4. Outside Block

5. Outside Knife Block

Overview

As outlined in the *Introduction* (page 10), Taekwondo is composed of five basic activities: the practice of fundamentals, self-defense, sport sparring, breaking, and forms. Part 2 of this book provided a brief overview of the basic elements that compose Taekwondo. In the author's larger book more than 380 strikes, blocks, and fundamental skills are covered. Part 3 describes how these basic techniques are combined for use in practical self-defense or combat.

In Taekwondo, self-defense practice involves training in specific unarmed techniques designed to protect oneself or others. Basic skills are combined and refined in a realistic context that approximates actual combat. This typically involves various forms of *sparring* (practice fighting) in which trainees perform prearranged actions, or learn to spontaneously improvise based on the changing dynamics of combat.

In Taekwondo, there are two basic modes that characterize self-defense: *attacking* and *counterattacking*. In attacking, you will decide when to initiate an offensive action. In counterattacking, you will respond based upon your opponent's actions. Most combat is essentially a blending of these two basic modes, with combatants shifting between offensive and defensive actions.

Attacking

Attacking is the art of seizing opportunity first. In self-defense sparring, attacking techniques are usually executed either by using explosive speed to hit your opponent before they can respond, or by feinting to set up an attack. A feint is an intentionally deceptive motion, designed to draw a particular response from your opponent, which you then exploit by executing a predetermined technique. When attacking, feinting is used to create an opening for a particular technique that might otherwise be blocked or countered. A common offensive feint is to make a striking motion with your lead hand or leg, and attack with your rear.

Counterattacking

In *counterattacking*, you will respond based upon your opponent's actions. You may react to an attack by executing a strike, block, or avoiding movement—or by responding with a combination of techniques (sequential or simultaneous). Counterattacks are launched either by *reacting* to an unknown attack, or by *feinting* to draw an opponent's attack (which you know is coming), leaving them vulnerable to your predetermined counterattack.

Taekwondo's Approach

Taekwondo's approach to actual self-defense is mostly characterized by counterattacking, although free-sparring practice commonly involves a balance of both attacking and counterattacking techniques. This emphasis on defense is said to be a reflection of Korea's long history of non-aggression toward its neighbors, with most of its military engagements being defensive actions against foreign aggressors. This defensive attitude is also a reflection of Taekwondo's long held belief that martial skills should only be used for the protection of oneself or others, or in organized sport competition.

Taekwondo does not possess a consistently well-defined body of self-defense techniques that are universally practiced throughout the art as a whole. In fact, specific self-defense techniques vary quite widely among individual schools. This is mostly because Taekwondo's self-defense skills are ultimately developed through free sparring. Because this method of practice encourages the development of improvisational skills, and a personalized approach to combat, it is only natural that Taekwondists would interpret and combine fundamental skills in unique and individual ways. Ideally, these personalized skills are an outgrowth of one's physique, natural abilities, and technical strengths and weaknesses.

Sparring Systems

In Taekwondo, self-defense training is defined by various forms of sparring, which generally fall into two basic categories: step sparring and self-defense sparring. In *step sparring*, trainees perform prearranged actions in a ritualized manner that is precisely defined. In *self-defense sparring*, trainees perform techniques in a more dynamic setting that involves either prearranged actions or free improvisation. These two basic categories of sparring are broken down as follows:

Step Sparring
- Three-Step Sparring
- Two-Step Sparring
- One-Step Sparring

Self-Defense Sparring
- Prearranged Sparring
- Free Sparring

Attacking (initiating an offensive action)

Counterattacking (responding to opponent's actions)

Step Sparring

Step sparring is a highly ritualized and controlled method of practice in which two trainees perform a series of predetermined offensive and defensive actions that involve little or no contact. All actions are determined and agreed upon beforehand, including footwork, target to be attacked, and strikes and blocks to be employed. Generally, the purpose of step sparring is to provide a safe setting in which novices can become comfortable with the concept of fighting, while also refining fundamentals and developing basic sparring skills, such as timing, balance, speed, power, concentration, emotional and physical control, and the ability to gauge distance. All step sparring begins with bows and other formal actions, including shouts to trigger the attack.

There are three basic types of step sparring: three-step, two step, and one-step. The differences between them are defined by the number of movements the trainees perform. Examples of these different systems are shown on the following pages.

Three-Step Sparring
Three-step sparring is the most basic form of step sparring and is often practiced by beginners. The attacker executes three strikes, stepping each time they strike. The defender blocks each strike, stepping each time they block. After the last block, the defender executes one or more counterstrikes. There are innumerable variations on this basic theme, based on the direction of the footwork and the strikes or blocks employed. In most cases, the attacker executes the same strike three times; typically, three punches to the same target or three kicks to the same target.

Two-Step Sparring
In two-step sparring, the attacker executes one punch and one kick while stepping. The defender blocks each strike, stepping each time they block. After the last block, the defender executes one or more counterstrikes. There are innumerable variations on this basic theme, based on the direction of the footwork and the strikes or blocks employed.

One-Step Sparring
In one-step sparring, the attacker executes one strike while stepping. The defender blocks and executes one or more counterstrikes. Traditionally, this was considered the most important form of step sparring, since it was felt to reflect the ultimate objective of actual self-defense: to end the fight quickly with a single decisive blow.

The Question of Value
Today, the value of step sparring is openly debated by many masters. Some feel that it provides a valuable method for introducing sparring to students who have a significant fear of physical contact or are extremely unathletic. Others feel that the traditional skills used in step sparring are obsolete and no longer reflect contemporary combat methods. Today, many styles no longer use this method of sparring, or primarily focus on one-step sparring drills consisting of modernized techniques.

Self-Defense Sparring

In self-defense sparring, the attacker executes any form of attack (strike, hold, throw), which the defender then counters. Self-defense sparring can involve either *prearranged sparring*, in which trainees perform predetermined actions; or *free sparring*, in which trainees must spontaneously improvise based on the changing dynamics of combat. In either method, techniques are usually executed in a dynamic setting that attempts to closely approximate real combat. This means the trainees are moving or shifting positions, operating from a variety of stances, and attacking without signaling their intent (no preliminary shout). Self-defense sparring typically involves either a single opponent, multiple opponents, or two defenders against two or more attackers.

Since most self-defense techniques can lead to serious injuries or death, it is necessary to take certain precautions in training to ensure the safety of trainees. Prearranged sparring is generally safer, since the offensive and defensive actions are predetermined. For this reason, it is usually preferred by individuals who enjoy a good workout, but wish to avoid the injuries that inevitably occur in free sparring. Ensuring safety in free sparring requires that trainees do one or more of the following: modify power, reduce contact, wear protective equipment, or agree to limit targets or responses. These restraints are very important, since accidental clashes can easily result in broken bones, a crushed windpipe, the loss of an eye, or other permanent or fatal injuries.

Techniques Shown in this Book

The techniques shown in *Part 3: Self-Defense* are representative of Taekwondo's basic approach to various self-defense situations. These techniques were selected from the 100-plus techniques documented in the author's 896-page Taekwondo book. These techniques are not meant to represent any particular style or federation, but to reflect the art of Taekwondo as a whole.

The 100-plus techniques shown in the larger book were selected based on practicality as well as concerns for preserving certain historical qualities unique to Taekwondo. Consequently, the techniques reflect both traditional and modernized approaches. Be aware that there are literally thousands of possible responses to any given situation. It is beyond the scope of any text to document all of these numerous possibilities.

Some of the self-defense techniques shown in the *Self-Defense Sparring* chapter have been extracted from sequences found in Taekwondo's forms, in order to illustrate the combat value that is often hidden in these patterns. Ultimately it is the manner in which you practice techniques, and the situations in which you use them, that largely determine their practicality, not the actual techniques themselves. Many of the techniques used in Olympic-Style competition (see Part 4), 140 of which are shown in the author's larger book, can also be adapted or modified for use in self-defense situations.

The following pages show six typical step-sparring sequences, selected from the 36-plus techniques contained in the author's 896-page Taekwondo book. Many other possibilities exist, since virtually any strike or block can be turned into a step-sparring drill. The techniques are organized in the three categories outlined previously: Three-Step Sparring, Two-Step Sparring, and One-Step Sparring. Each sequence is accompanied by a chart that summaries the attacker's and defender's actions. All step sparring begins in a formal manner

STEP SPARRING

that usually involves the following sequential steps: 1) the trainees face one another, come to Attention (Ch'aryŏt), bow (Kyŏngnye), and assume a Basic Ready Stance (Chunbi), with one trainee or a third party calling out the commands in parentheses; 2) the attacker steps back with one foot, as they execute a lead Low Block and Kihap (shout) to signal they are ready to attack; 3) the defender signals they are ready to defend with a Kihap; 4) the attacker strikes, the defender responds; 5) the trainees return to a Basic Ready Stance.

		Attacker	Defender
1. RLR High Lunge Punch *LRL Rising Block, R Reverse Punch*	A	R Forward Step into Front Stance R Lunge Punch (high)	R Back Step into Front Stance L Rising Block
	B	L Forward Step into Front Stance L Lunge Punch (high)	L Back Step into Front Stance R Rising Block
	C	R Forward Step into Front Stance R Lunge Punch (high)	R Back Step into Front Stance L Rising Block
	D	No action	R Reverse Punch (high)

Begin

A 1

A 2

B 1

B 2

C 1

C 2

D

Ready Stance

		Attacker	Defender
2. RLR High Lunge Punch *LRL Rising Block,* *R Rear Front Kick*	A	R Forward Step into Front Stance R Lunge Punch (high)	R Back Step into Front Stance L Rising Block
	B	L Forward Step into Front Stance L Lunge Punch (high)	L Back Step into Front Stance R Rising Block
	C	R Forward Step into Front Stance R Lunge Punch (high)	R Back Step into Front Stance L Rising Block
	D	No action	R Front Kick to belly or solar plexus (use rear leg) (if needed, slide lead-leg back to adjust range)

Begin

A 1

A 2

B 1

B 2

C 1

C 2

D 1

D 2

		Attacker	Defender
1. R Lunge Punch, L Front Kick *L Outside Block, X Block, R Lunge Punch*	A	R Forward Step into Front Stance R Lunge Punch (middle)	R Back Step into Front Stance L Outside Block
	B	L Front Kick to low section	L Back Step into Front Stance Low X Block
	C	Plant foot in lead position	Without stepping, R Lunge Punch to philtrum as attacker plants their foot

Ready Stance

Begin

A 1

A 2

B 1

B 2

C 1

C 2

		Attacker	Defender
2. R Rear Front Kick, Step, **L Side Punch** *R Low Block,* *L Outside Knife Block,* *L Lead Roundhouse Kick*	A	R Front Kick to low section (use rear leg)	L Back Step into Front Stance L Low Block (use rear hand)
	B	Plant foot in lead, L Forward Step into Riding Stance, L Side Punch	R Back Step into Tiger Stance L Outside Knife Block
	C	No action	L Roundhouse Kick to trunk or face (use lead leg)

Ready Stance

Begin

A 1

A 2

B 1

B 2

B 3

C 1

		Attacker	Defender
1. R Middle Lunge Punch *R Inside Block, R Downward Back Fist*	A	R Forward Step into Front Stance R Lunge Punch (middle)	R step forward into Riding Stance R Inside Block
	B	No action	R Downward Back Fist to philtrum

Ready Stance

Ready Stance

Begin

A 1

A 2

B 1

B 2

B 3

Ready Stance

		Attacker	Defender
2. L Middle Lunge Punch *R Jump Turning Back Kick*	A	L Forward Step into Front Stance L Lunge Punch (middle)	As attacker enters: step back with R foot, jump up and turn 180°, R Jump Back Kick to trunk or face

Ready Stance

Begin

A 1

A 2

A 3

The following pages show 14 typical self-defense sequences, selected from the 66-plus techniques contained in the author's 896-page Taekwondo book. Many other possibilities exist. Historically, self-defense techniques were not organized in any particular manner that was consistent across Taekwondo as a whole. To make it easier for the reader, this material will be organized and presented in specific categories. Some of the self-defense techniques shown in this chapter have been extracted from sequences found in Taekwondo's forms,

SELF-DEFENSE SPARRING

in order to illustrate the combat value that is often hidden in these patterns, all of which are documented in the author's 896-page book. Today the relative merits of traditional skills versus modern skills are vigorously debated. Recognize that the practicality of any technique is largely determined by the circumstances in which it is used. The important issue is not whether a given technique is old or new, but rather is it used in appropriate circumstances and applied proficiently. If it is, then its chances of success are much greater.

1. Against Lunge Punch

Inside Palm Block, 3 Punches, Knee Strike
From an open stance (A), the attacker shifts their lead foot forward and delivers a Lunge Punch. Step 45° forward with your lead foot, stepping to the attacker's outside as you deflect their punch with a lead Inside Palm Block (B). Without pausing, execute three straight punches in rapid succession: a Reverse Punch to the ribs (C), a Lunge Punch to the temple or jaw (D), and a Reverse Punch to the ribs (E). Follow up with a rear-leg Roundhouse Knee Strike (upward angle) or Front Knee Strike (forward thrust), depending on your orientation to your opponent.

Important Points
The punch combination should be very fast, and assisted by the turning motions of your hips. The punches can also be executed by stepping 45° forward into a Riding Stance (instead of a Front Stance) and punching with much less hip turn than shown in the photos. Alternating target height makes blocking more difficult. If desired, you can follow your knee strike with a Stamp Kick to the foot.

2. Against Front Kick

Low One-Knife Block, Arc Hand, Front Kick

From a closed stance (A), the attacker initiates a rear Front Kick (middle or low). Slide your rear foot backward (B), then withdraw your lead foot (Back Shuffle), weighting your rear leg as you execute a lead Low One-Knife Block (C). As the attacker plants forward, shift your lead foot into a Front Stance, as you execute a rear Arc Hand Strike to the cleft of the chin (breaks jaw) or throat (D). Leave your hand where it is, or drop your palm to the opponent's chest, and push them backward as you chamber your rear leg (E). Execute a Front Kick to the middle section (F).

Important Points

The attacker's plant carries them into your Arc Hand Strike, increasing the force of the blow. Time your push, chamber, and kick (D–F), so that you hit the opponent as they are knocked or pushed backward (F). Recognize that the force of your Arc Hand Strike may knock them backward, making an initial push unnecessary. This defense is found in the form *Koryŏ,* movements 9–10.

E (push and chamber)

1. Against Shoulder Grab

Outside One-Knife Block, Pulling Hammer Fist, Front Draw + Roundhouse Kick

An attacker standing to one side grips your shoulder or upper sleeve (A).Execute a forceful lead Outside One-Knife Block to nerves at their inner elbow, as you draw your rear fist backward (C). Your blow to the inner elbow bends the attacker's arm, brings their head forward, and may or may not release the hold. Immediately slip your lead hand to the back of the neck or rear-corner of the head, as you execute an Inside Hammer Fist Strike to the temple or jaw, pulling the head into the blow (D–E). Push the head away, as you slide your lead foot to your rear foot (to increase distance), chamber your rear leg, and execute a Roundhouse Kick to the head (F–G).

Important Points

The motion of the rear hand in step C can also be a Back Fist strike to an opponent standing on your other side or behind you. The first part of this defense (A–E) is based on movements 17–18 in the WTF form *Chit'ae*.

2. Against Two-Hand Collar Grab or Choke
Inner Spread Block, Palm Heel, Stretch Kick

From a relaxed stance (A), the attacker charges inward and attempts to grab your lapels or apply a choke with both hands. As they enter, step back with one foot into a Front Stance, so that you are in a closed stance relationship. At the same time, execute an Inner Spread Block, wedging their arms apart (A–B). Rapidly follow with a Front Palm Heel Strike to the chin (D). As the attacker is knocked backwards or retreats, chamber your rear leg (E) and execute a Stretch Kick, thrusting your Ball Foot or Sole Foot into the abdomen or solar plexus (F).

Important Points

This defense can also be used against a two-hand push. Note that the *Stretch Kick* is a forceful, thrusting strike (straight forward) that is different than a *Push Kick*. You can also substitute a Front Kick or a Side Kick, depending on distance. The first part of this defense (A–D) is based on movements 1–2 in the WTF form *Kŭmgang*. Note that the advancing footwork used in the form has been omitted for practical reasons.

1. Kneeling Lunge Punch

Rising Block, Pull + Lunge Punch, Pull + Chop

From a relaxed kneeling posture (A), the attacker steps forward with one foot and executes a Lunge Punch to your face. As soon as you detect motion, step forward with one foot into a closed stance relationship, as you execute a rear Rising Block (B–C). Grip their wrist with your rear hand and pull it toward your rear hip, as you execute a Lunge Punch to the philtrum (D). Retract your lead hand over your rear shoulder (E), then execute an Outside Knife Hand Strike to the side of the neck, as you pull the arm again (F).

Important Points

Pulling the opponent's arm (D, F) yanks them into your strike, and prevents them from using their held arm to block or strike. The formal kneeling posture from which this defense begins is common to many Asian cultures, and is typical of how these techniques were historically practiced in Taekwondo, as well as many other martial arts.

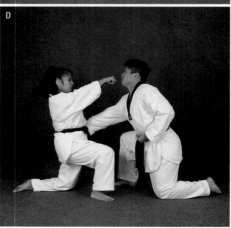

2. Kneeling Lunge Punch

Ground Roundhouse Kick

From a relaxed kneeling posture (A), the attacker steps forward with their right foot and executes a Lunge Punch to your face. As the punch is launched and the attacker steps forward, lean toward your left, plant your hands (B), chamber your right leg (C), and execute a Roundhouse Kick to the head (D). Steps B–D should performed in one rapid, continuous motion.

Important Points

Dropping and planting toward your left allows you to avoid the punch, and turns your hips to set up the kick. The kick can be executed with either the Ball Foot or Instep Foot. The formal kneeling posture from which this defense begins is common to many Asian cultures, and is typical of how these techniques were historically practiced in Taekwondo, as well as many other martial arts.

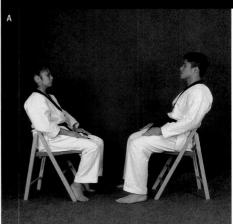

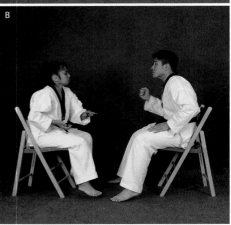

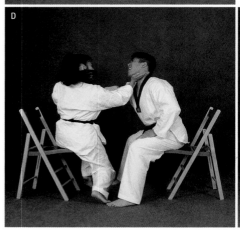

1. Seated Front Punch

Rising Block, Arm Pull/Twist,
Knife Hand Strike, Takedown

From a relaxed seated position (A), the attacker leans forward and punches to your face. As the punch is delivered, shift toward the attacker's inside, as you execute a Rising Block, grip the wrist, and chamber your Knife Hand (B). Pull and twist the attacker's arm toward your hip as you deliver an Inside Knife Hand Strike to the neck (D). Leave your hand on the neck or throat and continue to push the attacker sideways as you pull and twist their arm (E). This unbalances them sideways, forcing a fall (F). The *twisting* of the attacker's arm is important, since this causes them to lean sideways to relieve the joint lock, which assists your takedown.

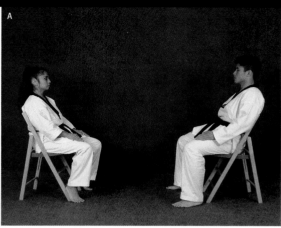

2. Standing Front Punch

Stand to Avoid, Outside Block,
Front Kick, Inside Elbow Strike

From a relaxed seated position (A), the attacker stands up and punches to your face. As the punch is delivered, shift toward the outside of the arm (B) and rise to a standing posture, as you execute an Outside Block while chambering your rear leg (C). Execute a Front Kick to the genitalia, hitting upward with your Instep Foot (D). Plant your foot laterally, in front of the attacker. At the same time, grip their wrist with your blocking hand and pull it forward and downward to expose their head, as you execute an Inside Elbow Strike to the jaw or temple (E). Use the forward momentum of your foot plant, and your hip and shoulder rotation, to power the elbow strike.

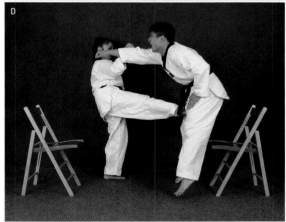

1. Against Multiple Opponents

Two opponents attack simultaneously with a high straight punch and a low or middle Roundhouse Kick. Shift into a right Front Stance (facing rearward) as you execute a High-Low Block, using your forearms to deflect the blows (A–B). As the left-attacker plants forward, shift your left foot sideways, pivot 180°, and assume a left Front Stance as you execute a Reverse Punch to the solar plexus (C). Note that the lateral shifting of your head and upper body allows you to avoid the right-attacker's second punch, while the left-attacker's forward momentum carries them into your punch. Slide your right foot toward your left foot to adjust your distance, as you chamber your left leg (D) and execute a left Back Kick to the right-attacker's ribs, solar plexus, or head (E).

2. Against Multiple Opponents

Two attackers are standing 180° opposed. One grabs clothing at your shoulder, as the other executes a lead straight punch to your head (A). Shift into a left Back Stance and deflect the punch with a left Outside Block, as you deliver a right Rising-Circular Back Fist Strike to the philtrum or face of the attacker behind you (B). The left-attacker immediately follows their lead punch with a rear straight punch. Deflect the blow with a left Downward Palm Block, as you execute a right Front Back Fist Strike to their philtrum (C). Chamber your right leg and execute a Back Kick to the right-attacker's midsection (D). Plant your foot in the rear position, assuming a left Walking Stance as you grip the back of the left-attacker's head with both hands (E). Execute a right Rising Knee Strike to their face (F).

1. Downward Club Strike

Rising One-Knife Block, Pull + Arc Hand Strike, Takedown, Downward Punch

From a closed stance (A), the attacker steps forward with their rear foot and delivers a downward strike with a club. As soon as you detect the attack, step 45° forward with your lead foot, to the attacker's outside. Execute a lead Rising One-Knife Block to the forearm or wrist. Grip the wrist and twist it as you pull it downward and sideways, unbalancing the opponent toward their side or rear-corner. At the same time, execute an Arc Hand Strike to the throat, clamping it tightly (C). Step forward with your rear foot and plant it behind the attacker's lead foot, as you push against their throat (D) to force a fall (E). As they land, execute a Downward Punch to the groin, solar plexus or face (F).

2. Downward Knife Strike

Rising Block + Reverse Punch, Jump Side Kick

From an open stance (A), the attacker executes a downward thrust. As soon as you detect the attack, charge inward, stepping to the attacker's outside as you execute a lead Rising Block to the triceps tendon (just below the point of the elbow), and a simultaneous Reverse Punch to the ribs (D). Without pausing, jump backward toward your closed side, chamber your legs (E–F), and execute a Jump Side Kick to the armpit, upper arm, trunk, or ribs (G).

Important Points

When initially stopping the strike, blocking to the attacker's wrist or forearm is not recommended, since you can easily be cut and it is more difficult to control the attacker's arm. When executing the jump kick, you will jump to the attacker's outside, since it is generally considered to be a safer position.

1. Lunge-Reverse Punches, Sweep Kick

From a closed stance (A), quickly slide your lead foot forward as you execute a Lunge Punch to the philtrum (B), rapidly followed by a Reverse Punch to the solar plexus (C–D). Quickly chamber your rear leg and execute a Sweep Kick to the lead ankle or a Roundhouse Kick to the back or side of the lead knee (E), sweeping the opponent's lead leg out from under them. This usually results in a fall (F).

Important Points

The first punch will likely be blocked; however, its purpose is mostly to set up the second and/or third technique by drawing the opponent's defense to a high attack. In this sequence of blows, the rapid alteration in target height and distance puts a greater burden on the opponent's defense. Speed and properly timing the initial strike are fundamentally important. Try to launch the combination after executing preliminary feints to disrupt your opponent's timing, or at a moment when your opponent seems tentative, confused, or inattentive. This generally applies to most attacking techniques.

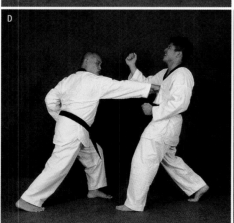

2. Forward Slide, Pressing Knife Kick, Turning Hook Kick

From an open stance (A), spring forward, sliding your rear foot toward your lead foot as you chamber your lead leg (B). Execute a lead Pressing Knife Kick to the lead knee (C). Your opponent reacts to the blow or avoids it, by executing a Back Slide (D). Quickly plant your lead foot forward, as you turn 180° toward your posterior side, chamber your rear leg (E), and deliver a Turning Hook Kick to the head using the Back Heel (F).

Important Points

After your kick to the knee, the placement of your lead-foot plant is based upon how far your opponent moves. For example, if they don't move much, plant near your rear foot. If you need to cover greater distance, plant more forward. The Turning Hook Kick is a very fast and powerful blow, capable of producing devastating injuries. If it is thrown slowly or awkwardly (as often seen in motion pictures and on television), it is easily avoided or countered. This kick can also be applied using the Sole Foot.

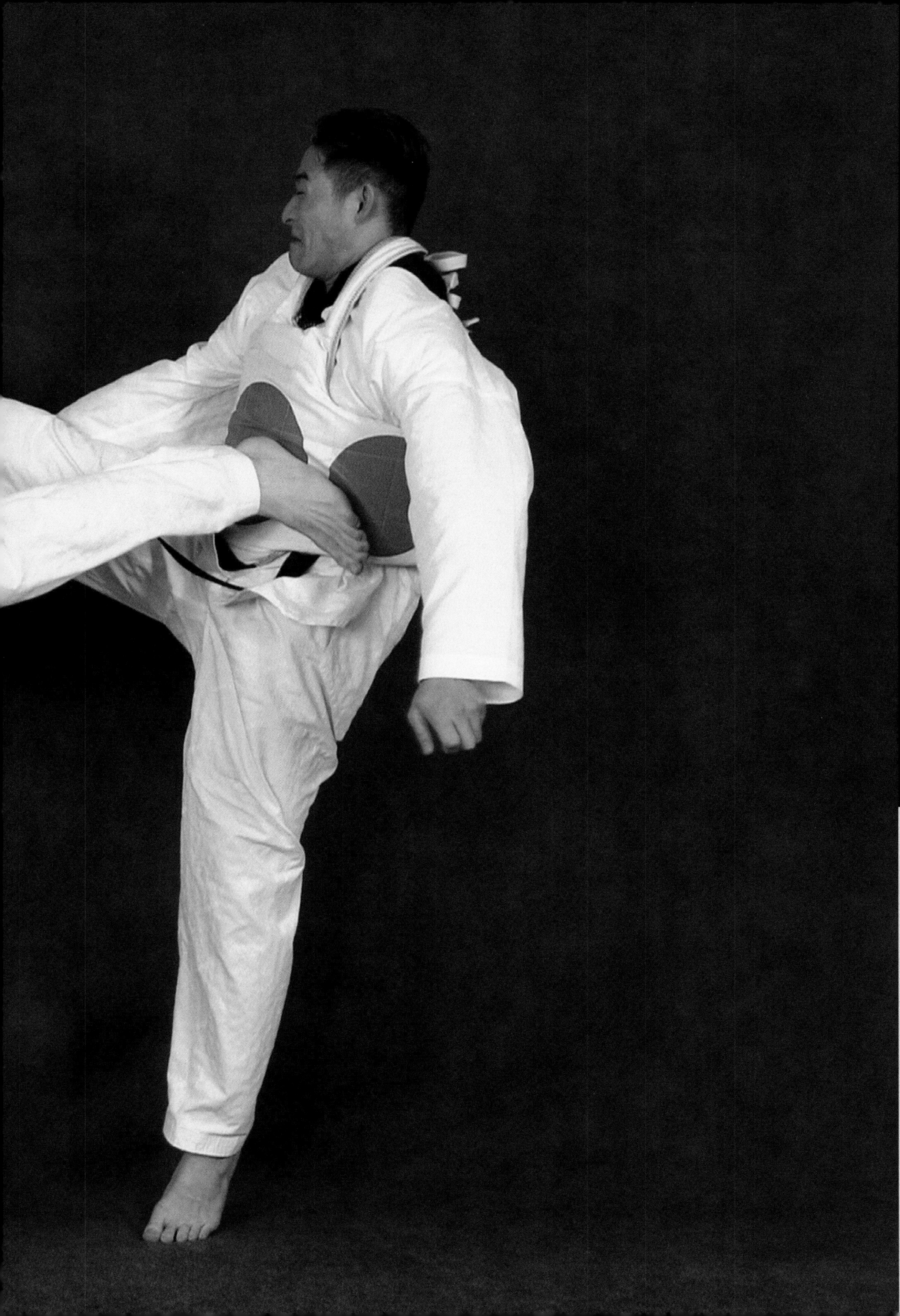

PART 4

OLYMPIC-STYLE

Overview

As outlined in the *Introduction* (page 10), Taekwondo is composed of five basic activities: the practice of fundamentals, self-defense, sport sparring, breaking, and forms. The purpose of competitive sport sparring is to: 1) hold a contest of skills based on specific rules in which the competitors and spectators can enjoy the act of winning and losing; 2) provide a forum in which one can test and evolve skills, with less risk of injury than real combat permits; and 3) provide an activity that promotes the cultivation of positive moral values and character qualities that are an essential part of other aspects of life—qualities such as inner strength, resiliency, confidence, assertiveness, and the ability to triumph over adversity, accept defeat graciously, and never give up. Of the various forms of competitive sport sparring found in Taekwondo as a whole, *Olympic-Style sparring* is unarguably the most popular and widely practiced sport application. Since Olympic-Style Taekwondo has developed along very specific lines, often in marked contrast to other styles of Taekwondo, the author's 896-page Taekwondo book contains a comprehensive 156-page overview of the principles, current trends, and techniques that define Olympic-Style sport competition. More than 140 techniques are shown in detail, some of which are on the following pages.

What is Olympic-Style?

Olympic-Style sparring is a global competitive sport in which two competitors attempt to score points by kicking and punching one another at prescribed targets above the waist. Full-contact is permitted, much like boxing, with competitors wearing protective body armor and mouth guards to reduce the likelihood of injury. The person who scores the most points after three rounds wins. Matches are also won by knockout, or when another fighter can no longer continue. At this time, Olympic-Style competition consists almost entirely of kicking techniques. While punches will occasionally be awarded points, they are mostly used for other tactical reasons (e.g., feints, checks, create space, move opponent).

Olympic-Style sparring evolved during the latter 1970s under the guidance of the World Taekwondo Federation in South Korea, and became a demonstration sport at the 1988 Seoul Olympic Games. It remained an Olympic demonstration sport (except for 1996) until the 2000 Sydney Olympic Games, at which time it became a permanent Olympic event. Olympic-Style Taekwondo has evolved according to very specific rules governing competition. The body of skills used in Olympic-Style sparring is a small fraction of the techniques contained in Taekwondo as a whole.

Sport vs Martial Art

Today, the rapid growth of sport Taekwondo is seen as having both positive and negative impact on the art as a whole. On the positive side, sport Taekwondo is one of the major factors contributing to Taekwondo's growth worldwide, and has brought tremendous numbers of youths and families into the martial arts. On the negative side, Olympic-Style Taekwondo is seen as one of the greatest threats to Taekwondo's ability to remain a true martial art, incorporating character development and practical self-defense skills. This is largely due to the narrowly focused sport emphasis that increasingly characterizes many schools today, as well as the differing objectives of sport and self-defense. These issues and others are dealt with in greater detail in the *Introduction* chapter of the author's 896-page book.

Competition Setting

Olympic-Style competition occurs within a 10 by 10 meter (32.8 by 32.8 foot) square area, between two competitors attempting to score points by kicking or punching legal targets. Each competitor must wear approved uniforms and protective gear, including head gear, mouth piece, trunk guard, shin guards, forearm guards, and a groin guard. The trunk guard is color-coded blue (*ch'ŏng*) or red (*hong*) to distinguish one competitor from the other. Competitors are divided into divisions according to gender, weight, age, and experience (belt rank). A match consists of three rounds. Each round is three minutes,

with a one minute break between rounds, and is typically regulated by a referee and three judges. The winner is usually determined by points or knockout. Olympic-Style competition is governed by a specific body of rules, established and periodically amended by an international governing association, the World Taekwondo Federation (WTF). Generally, the key factors are:

- Kicks can be executed to the head (in front of the ears) and trunk (areas covered by trunk guard), using any part of the foot below the ankle.
- Fore Fist punches can be executed only to the trunk (areas covered by trunk guard); other types of hand strikes are prohibited.
- No punches to the head.
- No strikes below belt level.
- No holding or throwing techniques.
- Mandatory protective equipment.
- Point scoring is based on target, technique, and proper hitting power.

Violations of the rules result in warnings, point deductions, or disqualification, based on the type of offense. Recognize that most competitors will try to stretch the rules as far as possible. For example, hitting below the waist is not allowed; however, it is currently common for Push Kicks (also called *Cut Kicks*) to be directed to the upper thigh, without being penalized.

Weight Divisions				
	Male		*Female*	
Fin	- 54kg	(118.8)	- 47kg	(103.4)
Fly*	- 58kg	(127.6)	- 51kg	(112.2)
Bantam	- 62kg	(136.4)	- 55kg	(121.0)
Feather*	- 67kg	(147.4)	- 59kg	(129.8)
Light	- 72kg	(158.4)	- 63kg	(138.6)
Welter*	- 78kg	(171.6)	- 67kg	(147.4)
Middle	- 84kg	(182.6)	- 72kg	(158.4)
Heavy*	+84kg	(182.6)	+72kg	(158.4)

Eight weight divisions are typically used for adult black-belt competitions (pounds in parenthesis). The Olympic Games use 4 divisions (*) formed by combining two adjoining classes (e.g., Fin-Fly, Bantam-Feather, etc.). Note that weight limits and competition rules change periodically. The most recent updates can be found at the USTU's website: www.ustu.org

Competition Area

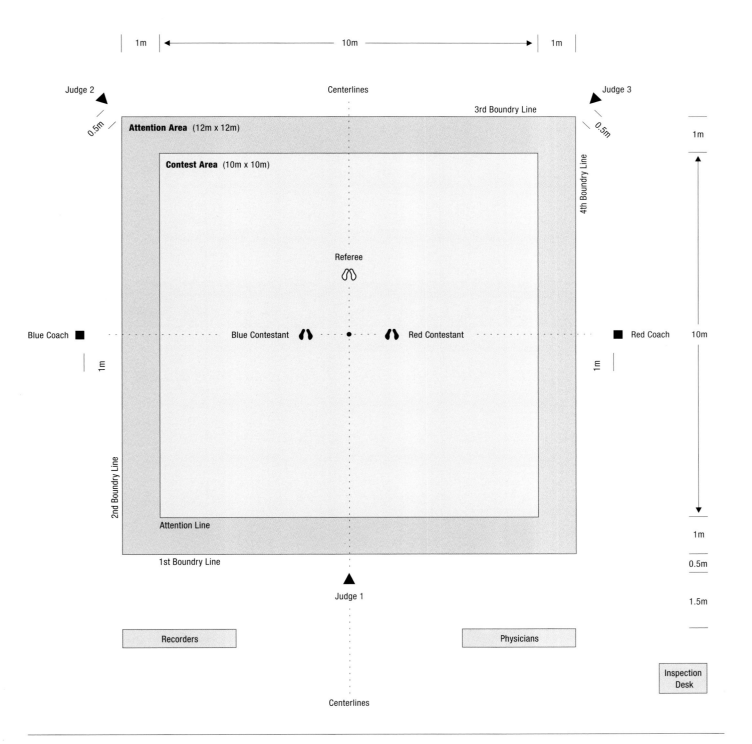

1m ←————— 10m —————→ 1m

Judge 2

Centerlines

3rd Boundry Line

Judge 3

0.5m

Attention Area (12m x 12m)

0.5m

1m

Contest Area (10m x 10m)

4th Boundry Line

Referee

Blue Coach

Blue Contestant   Red Contestant

Red Coach

10m

1m

1m

2nd Boundry Line

Attention Line

1m

1st Boundry Line

0.5m

Judge 1

1.5m

Recorders

Physicians

Inspection
Desk

Centerlines

In Olympic-Style sparring, technique evolves according to the demands of competition; self-defense and practical combat are of no concern. When compared to Taekwondo as a whole, Olympic-Style uses a smaller number of techniques that have been refined to a much higher degree. These techniques continue to evolve according to what works and scores points within the highly regulated environment of sport competition. Some of the techniques that are very popular today will likely fall out of favor in the coming years.

ATTACKS + COUNTERS

Some of those skills that have fallen out of favor often reappear years later incorporating new innovations. It is important to realize that recommended methods and techniques are constantly evolving and changing. There are also many individuals who adopt unorthodox techniques or tactics that work well for them. The following pages show typical attacking and counterattacking techniques, selected from the author's 896-page book. They are grouped based on how the competitors are oriented, either in open stances or closed stances.

1. Lead Roundhouse Kick, Rear Double Roundhouse

From a closed stance (A), spring forward, sliding your rear foot toward your lead foot (B), as you chamber your lead leg. As your rear foot plants, execute a lead Roundhouse Kick to the body (C). If the opponent reacts with a Back Slide as you hit and retract (D), plant your foot forward. If they remain stationary, shift backward by planting your lead foot near your rear foot as your rear foot slides back. Without pausing, chamber your rear foot

(F), and execute a rear Roundhouse Kick to the ribs, or the back of the thigh or buttock (G). Quickly retract the kick as you spring off your support foot, chamber your leg, turn your body (H), and deliver a Roundhouse Kick to the body or head, on the open side (I). The foot-plant forward (D–E), is used to maintain the proper distance to set up the Double Roundhouse. This three-kick attack can also be executed by initiating the second kick as you retract your lead leg, before planting the foot, in which case it is a *Triple Roundhouse*.

Common Counters
When launching this attack, be aware that the following counters are often employed:

- Jump Back Kick (on fist kick)
- Back Slide, Back Kick
- Back Slide, Front Draw, rear Roundhouse
- Step forward and clinch
- Back Slide, lead Downward Kick (on second kick)

2. Fast Cut Kick, Jump Back Kick

From a closed stance (A), spring forward, sliding your rear foot toward your lead foot, as you lift your lead leg (B–C). Deliver a lead Cut Kick to the lead thigh or hip (D). As you kick, your opponent Back Slides to avoid it, immediately launching a Double Roundhouse as you plant your foot (E). Spring upward, turn 180° toward your posterior side (F), chamber your rear leg (G), and extend your foot straight backward, delivering a Back Kick to the body, on the open side (H–I). Note that both of the Roundhouses hit your closed side (no points).

Important Points
This attack works well, whether your opponent reacts as in the previous attack or counters with the Double Roundhouse. The key factor in neutralizing the Double Roundhouse is your body turn, which ensures that your closed side is turning toward each kick. The first kick will likely hit you in the buttocks (F); the second on your hip or backside. Neither of these are scoring blows. Upon finishing the Back Kick, quickly retract your foot and plant it forward, stepping close to the opponent to hinder counterkicks (I).

Common Counters
When launching this attack, be aware that the following counters are often employed:

- Back Slide, Lead Double Roundhouse (during turn)
- Back Slide, lead Roundhouse Kick (before turn)
- Back Slide, Turning Whip Kick
- Back Slide, Turning Hook Kick

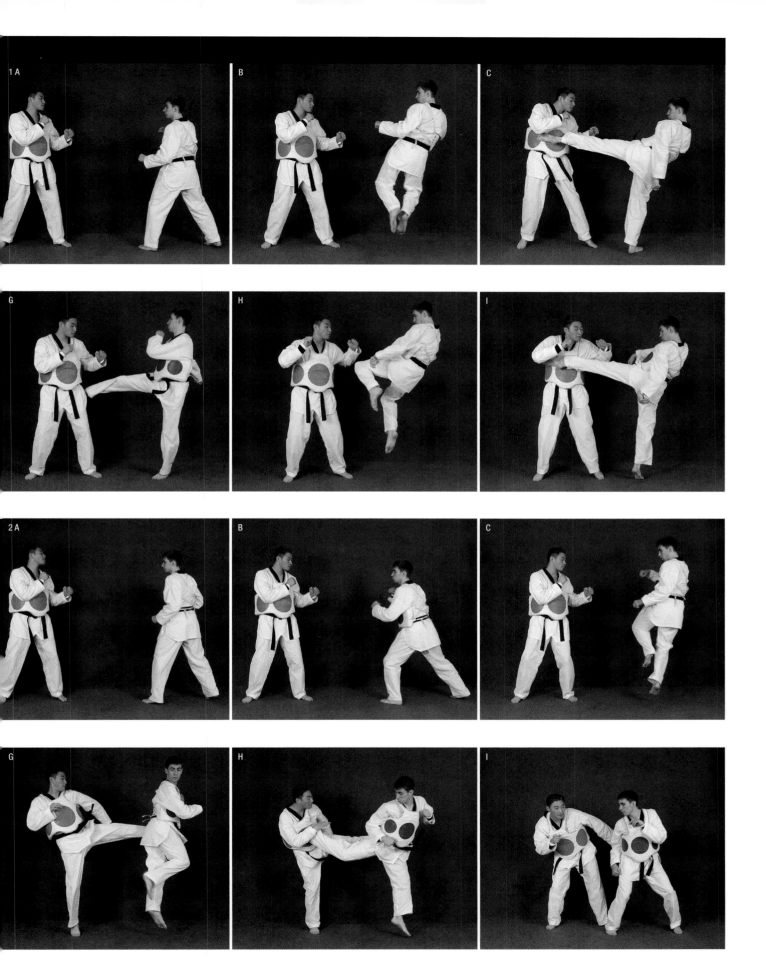

1. Rear Roundhouse Kick

This technique is used to launch a rear Roundhouse Kick to the open side, when you are already within range. From an open stance (A), push off with the rear foot (B), chamber your rear leg (C), and execute a Roundhouse Kick to the body (D). Quickly retract the kick (E) and plant your foot forward, stepping close to the opponent (F). Stepping close makes it difficult for your opponent to quickly initiate a counterkick, since they must first move farther away to achieve the proper distance.

Important Points

This attack is usually launched as an opponent steps forward within range; or by spot shifting or stepping into position. Recognize that either competitor can attack from this range (A), so you must strike very quickly or change distance. The rear Roundhouse Kick is one of the most widely used forms of attack in Olympic-Style sparring. It is also a fundamental kick used to launch many combinations, such as the Double Roundhouse Kick shown on the previous pages.

Common Counters

When launching this attack, be aware that the following counters are often employed:

- Jump Back Kick
- Turning Whip Kick
- Double Roundhouse Kick
- Cover-Punch, Roundhouse Kick
- Reverse Turning Roundhouse Kick
- Lead Roundhouse Kick
- Rear Downward Kick
- Cut Kick, Jump Back Kick

2. Forward Step, Back Kick

This attack is used to quickly move closer as you launch a Back Kick to the open side. Adjust the length of your initial step based on the distance you need to cover. From an open stance (A), step forward with your rear foot (B), turn 180° toward your posterior side (C), and chamber your rear leg (D). Drop your arm downward for cover as you extend your leg straight backward, delivering a Back Kick to the body, on the open side (E). Quickly retract the kick and plant the foot forward, close to your opponent, to hinder counterkicks (F).

Important Points

The initial Forward Step can be used to move substantially closer, within kicking distance, or to chase down an opponent who habitually retreats. Stepping and kicking should be executed in one continuous, explosive motion. As you step forward, use your momentum and rotational force to launch and power your rear-leg kick. Try to hit your opponent before they can move or while they are still stepping. This disrupts their balance and timing, and reduces the likelihood that you will be hit by a counterkick.

Common Counters

When launching this attack, be aware that the following counters are often employed:

- Long Back Slide, rear Roundhouse Kick
- Lead Push Kick, Lead Double Roundhouse
- Step 45°, Roundhouse to face (from rear)
- Step 45°, Double Roundhouse

1. Against Lead Roundhouse Kick

Back Slide, Lead Roundhouse Kick

From a closed stance (A), execute a Back Slide to avoid the attacker's Forward Slide and lead Roundhouse Kick (B–C). As they plant their kicking foot, lift your lead foot, chamber the leg (D), and execute a lead Roundhouse Kick to the body (E). Quickly retract the kick and plant your foot forward, stepping close to the opponent (F). Stepping close makes it difficult for your opponent to quickly initiate counters without first moving farther away.

Important Points

Always be ready to block with your arm, in case you are unable to avoid the kick. When stepping backward, move only far enough to avoid the kick. If you step too much, you will be too far away to hit your opponent. If you need to increase your kick's range slightly, hop or slide on your supporting leg as you deliver the kick. Note that the support foot is fully turned (D–E). To generate sufficient scoring power, this kick is usually thrown more horizontal than most Roundhouse Kicks.

2. Drawing and Counterattacking

Lead Step (feint), Rear Downward Kick

From a closed stance (A), slide your lead foot forward, faking a rear-leg attack (B). Your opponent reacts with a rear kick (if they don't react, retract your lead foot to its original position). On their motion, chamber your rear leg (C). Thrust your foot forward and upward (D), then pull it forcefully downward into the opponent's face (E). Step forward toward the opponent as you plant your foot, to discourage counters (F). If your Downward Kick misses, step close and clinch.

Important Points

Your initial lead step forward is not only used to draw the attack, but to position you closer for your Downward Kick. Otherwise, you will be too far away when you kick. It is important to initiate an explosive counterattack at the moment your opponent makes a motion to launch a rear-leg attack. Your intention is to hit them while they are still chambering or extending their leg (D–E). This allows you to hit them as they move forward into your kick. If they do get a Roundhouse off, be prepared to block with your arm (E).

1. Against Rear Roundhouse

Jump Back Kick

From an open stance (A), the attacker initiates a rear Roundhouse Kick. As they kick (B), spring upward, turn 180° toward your posterior side, and chamber your rear leg (C–D). Drop your arm for cover as you extend your foot straight backward, delivering a Back Kick to the body, on the opponent's open side (E). Quickly retract your kick and plant your foot forward, stepping close to the opponent to make further attacks more difficult (F).

Important Points

The key factor in neutralizing your opponent's Roundhouse is to make a fast body-turn. This ensures that your closed side is turning toward their kick, so your scoring targets are covered. In step E, the Roundhouse hits your closed side, failing to score. A quick turn also makes it more difficult for your opponent to avoid the Back Kick, since they are still committed to finishing their Roundhouse. Try to hit them while they are still supported on one leg (E), possibly causing a fall.

2. Against Lead Double Roundhouse

Rear Roundhouse, Cover-Punch

From an open stance (A), the attacker initiates a Forward Slide and lead Double Roundhouse. On their motion, push off with your rear foot and chamber your rear leg (B). Cover with your arm as you execute a rear Roundhouse to the body, on the open side (C). As you plant forward, the attacker immediately initiates the second kick (D). Execute a Cover-Punch, blocking their leg with your lead arm, as you punch their chest with your rear fist (E). Deflect the leg outward, unbalancing them.

Important Points

In this counter, you will kick first to score, then neutralize the second kick. Launch your counterkick as soon as you detect your opponent's motion, trying to beat their first kick whenever possible. If you are too late, the second kick may hit you before you can get off the Cover-Punch. When executing the Cover-Punch, try to lean forward and shift your body closer: the closer you are, the more difficult it will be for your opponent to hit you. If you can catch them in the air (E), it will be easier to unbalance them.

D

E

F

D

E

F

Overview

As outlined in the *Introduction* (page 10), Taekwondo is composed of five basic activities: the practice of fundamentals, self-defense, sport sparring, breaking, and forms. Breaking (called *kyŏkp'a* in Korean) is an activity in which the Taekwondoist attempts to break different materials—such as wood, concrete, granite, brick, and glass—by using specific striking techniques. Breaking techniques, often noted for their spectacular effect, are not practiced to impress people, but to perfect crucial aspects of striking, such as proper hand/foot formation, speed, power, penetration, timing, accuracy, concentration, breathing, and mind-body-spirit harmony. Breaking also provides a socially acceptable forum for practicing deadly, full-power blows.

Any attack point (body surface you hit with) can be used for breaking, although some are more suitable or safer than others, based on their ability to sustain impact without damage. This is mostly determined by the degree of power you use and the characteristics of the material you are trying to break. Virtually any striking technique can be used for breaking, and might encompass punches, open hand strikes, fingertip thrusts, elbow strikes, and kicks. An overview of materials, training concerns, and over 20 typical breaks is found in the author's 896-page Taekwondo book.

A Word of Caution

Unfortunately, continued breaking will likely lead to damage to nerves, ligaments, tendons, joints, and bone, which can lead to significant long-term negative health effects, such as constant pain, chronic inflammation, loss of dexterity, loss of muscle strength, arthritis, and bone cancer. Breaking should only be learned and practiced under the supervision of a qualified master, and with the full knowledge that you may adversely affect your health. The purpose of the material in this chapter is to outline the parameters that define *breaking*. The techniques shown on these pages are done by experts with substantial training. Do not attempt to learn these techniques from these illustrations.

Basic Concepts

While there are many different types of breaking techniques, virtually all are defined by three essential qualities: speed, power, and penetration. The differences between different breaking techniques are usually defined by the degree to which they emphasize one or more of these qualities.

Speed Breaks

Speed breaks are breaking techniques that primarily depend on the velocity of your hand or foot to break the material. Power and penetration are also important, but much less so. In speed breaks, the material to be broken is usually suspended in such a way that it will easily move away when struck: the material may be hanging from string, loosely held at one end, freestanding, or tossed up in the air and hit while airborne. In all cases, the strike must be fast enough to shatter the material before it can move away. The method of support and the characteristics of the breaking

material (e.g., surface hardness, flexibility, weight, thickness, density, tensile strength, etc.) determine the degree of difficulty and speed requirements. For example, it is usually easier to break a board held at one end, than one that is tossed up and struck while airborne. A speed break is shown below.

Power Breaks

Power breaks are breaking techniques that primarily depend on the power you generate in your strike to break the chosen material. This material is usually firmly supported in such a way that it will not move away when struck. This usually means the material is supported at either end, usually by individuals who function as holders, or by placing the material on a stable, rigid platform. The degree of difficulty and power requirements of a specific break are determined by the quantity of material, method of support (degree of rigidity), and the characteristics of the breaking material (surface hardness,

Speed Breaks (techniques that mostly depend on velocity)

flexibility, weight, thickness, density, tensile strength, etc.). For example, it is easier to break one single board than four boards stacked together. It is easier to break boards placed on a rigid platform than boards held by people, since the platform doesn't give, whereas people absorb some of the force by their movements during impact. When breaking with hand strikes, it is usually easier to break by hitting downward than by hitting horizontally, since downward strikes allow you to use the entire weight of your dropping body to add power to the blow. An example of a power break is shown below.

Penetration Breaks
Penetration breaks are breaking techniques that primarily depend on sustained speed and power to break the chosen material. Typically, several pieces of breaking material are supported on a platform, with small spacers placed between each piece. When the stack of material is struck, the pieces will break

sequentially. In order to break all the pieces, the breaker must be able to maintain speed and power until their blow has penetrated to the last piece. The degree of difficulty and penetration requirements of a specific break are mostly determined by the quantity of material, the characteristics of the breaking material, and the method of support (degree of rigidity). Depth of penetration is mostly judged by the the number of pieces. Naturally, greater penetration is required to break twelve boards with spacers than four boards with spacers. Breaks without spacers require greater power, whereas breaks with spacers require greater penetration. An example of a penetration break is shown below.

Speed vs Power
Speed and power requirements in breaking are largely determined by how rigidly the material is supported. The more easily the material moves under impact, the more speed is required. It is common for people to blame

the movement of their holders for a failure to break; however, more speed on their part would negate the holder's natural motions.

Mental Aspects of Breaking
As previously outlined in the *Philosophy* chapter, Taekwondo strikes are characterized by the proper use of physics, concentration of power through the use of one's entire body, breath control, and the total commitment of one's mind, body, and spirit. Nowhere are these principles more concretely tested than in breaking. Any technical error, lapse in concentration, or crisis of confidence can easily result in serious injury. For this reason, proper mental centering is essential, before executing any difficult or dangerous break. What constitutes "difficult" or "dangerous" will of course vary widely based on the skill and experience of each individual. For this reason, it is important that you possess a realistic view of your own limitations. Unjustified confidence only leads to injury.

Power Breaks (techniques that mostly depend on power)

Penetration Breaks (techniques that mostly depend on sustained speed and power)

Overview

As outlined in the *Introduction* (page 10), Taekwondo is composed of five basic activities: the practice of fundamentals, self-defense, sport sparring, breaking, and forms. Forms (called *Hyŏng, P'umsae, or T'ŭl* in Korean) are solo exercises in which the Taekwondoist practices a predetermined pattern of movements and techniques, against imaginary opponents. Forms are used to ingrain basic motions and combinations; develop speed, fluidity, timing, power, strength, endurance, and proper breathing; sharpen concentration; and build conditioned responses to various forms of attacks and counterattacks. Once a form has been memorized and deeply embedded into one's being, it can also be used as a form of moving meditation, to refine one's spiritual qualities. This aspect of forms training was covered in Part 2, under *Breathing + Meditation*.

One of the advantages of forms training is that it does not require a partner and can be practiced anywhere there is sufficient space. For some individuals, forms training also helps alleviate the boredom that can come from the constant repetition of basic motions. Forms can also be practiced when you are too old, too young, or too injured to engage in sparring or other contact activities.

Historical Origins

Historically, forms training evolved as a method for warriors to ingrain lethal skills necessary for their survival in combat, without having to practice on one another. In ancient times, safe methods of free sparring did not yet exist and most combat focused on the use of weapons. Most skills were refined through the repetitive practice of fundamental motions and the cumulative experience gained in warfare. Naturally, this was not an environment in which one could "learn from their mistakes," since most errors were usually fatal. When the concept of forms training first evolved, it must have been viewed as an important innovation, since it served as an invaluable bridge between the practice of fundamentals and lethal combat.

In forms training, warriors could practice lethal skills against several imaginary opponents, without lethal consequences.

After the advent of free sparring and protective equipment in the twentieth century, forms training became more valued as a form of moving meditation, and as a complementary training method for refining breathing, concentration, and basic biomechanical motions—aspects of training that tended to get submerged during free sparring. Today this is a great deal of debate among Taekwondoists, some of whom question the usefulness of forms and their current relevancy to modern sport and self-defense. These issues are discussed in the *Introduction* of the author's 896-page Taekwondo book.

Systems of Forms

As Taekwondo emerged in the mid-twentieth century, many of the early kwans established their own sets of forms. Some of these forms were merely adopted from older foreign styles; others were attempts to integrate native Korean skills. Some of the sets of forms that evolved were infused with philosophical or aesthetic ideas intended to tie them to Korean cultural traditions.

Today the specific sets of forms being practiced vary widely, depending on the style of Taekwondo one practices. Unfortunately, there are far too many different forms in existence for it to be practical to outline them all. It is also not particularly useful, since many are very similar to one another, or are derived from foreign forms common to other martial arts. The forms selected for inclusion in the author's 896-page book are those most widely observed today in mainstream Taekwondo. In that book, forms are organized into four categories, each of which constitutes a separate chapter:

• P'algwae Forms
• T'aegŭk Forms
• WTF Black Belt Forms
• ITF Patterns

Within these four systems, forms are graded in terms of their difficulty. The specific form(s) one practices is usually based on one's skill and rank. Generally, most martial artists will judge a form's worth based on its difficulty, complexity, technical variety, aesthetic merits, and the degree to which it accurately reflects both actual combat and the technical nature of a martial art. The linear pattern that a specific form makes when viewed from overhead is referred to as the form's "line" or "pattern."

P'algwae Forms

The P'algwae series, which emerged in the early 1970s, consists of eight forms that are typically associated with the colored grades occurring before black belt. *P'al-gwae* ("eight trigrams") is a term derived from ancient East Asian cosmology, which refers to the eight primary combinations of yin and yang forces (see *Philosophy* chapter, "Law of Change"). Some practitioners will use this philosophical underpinning as a guide when using these forms for moving meditation, although there has has never been any clearly defined or established framework by which this is done. Each P'algwae form is referred to as a *"chang"* (meaning "section" or "chapter"); for example, "P'algwae 1 Chang." All eight forms comprise a complete set, technically and philosophically; and each individual form is a part of that set, much like the chapters in a book. The same is also true of the eight T'aegŭk forms described next.

T'aegŭk Forms

The T'aegŭk series consists of eight forms that are typically associated with the colored grades occurring before black belt. *T'ae-gŭk* ("supreme ultimate") is the Korean name for the yin-yang symbol, which depicts the two great forces of the universe in perfect balance and perpetual alteration. Like the P'algwae forms, each of the eight T'aegŭk forms is associated with one of the eight primary combinations of yin and yang forces as represented by the eight trigrams (see *Philosophy* chapter, "Law of Change"). The linear pattern of each form is based on the shape of the Chinese character for "king."

The T'aegŭk series emerged in the 1970s (after the P'algwaes) under the World Taekwondo Federation (WTF), allegedly out of a need for forms that: reflected more modern methods of combat; more closely mirrored the philosophical ideas behind the eight trigrams; and used technical elements more indicative of Taekwondo and native Korean skills. Whether they accomplish this is a subject widely debated. Some Taekwondoists feel that these forms were poorly conceived and lack practical value; others like them and appreciate their modernity. Generally, the T'aegŭk forms use short stances and motions more typical of modern combat, whereas the P'algwae series uses deep stances and long motions more typical of traditional fighting. The T'aegŭk series was intended to replace the P'algwaes; however, both sets of forms are still widely practiced at this time.

Some Korean masters have articulated elaborate philosophical constructs that allegedly underpin each of the eight T'aegŭk forms, which are intended to guide one's mental-spiritual approach to forms practice. However, when these concepts are compared to the actual physical movements within the forms, their connection is tenuous at best.

WTF Black Belt Forms

This series consists of nine forms intended to be practiced by black belt ranks. The creation of these forms was initiated in the mid 1960s by the Korea Taekwondo Association, and subsequently finalized under the WTF. The linear pattern of each form is based on a different Chinese or Korean character, which represents an underlying philosophical principle behind the form.

ITF Patterns

This series consist of 24 forms encompassing colored grades and black belt ranks. The forms first began to emerge in the 1950s under the direction of the notable pioneer, Hong-Hi Choi, who referred to them as "patterns." The name, number of movements, and diagrammatic symbol for each pattern symbolizes notable individuals or events in Korean history. This series of forms is commonly associated with the International Taekwon-do Federation (ITF), although they are also widely practiced by Taekwondoists who are not affiliated with this association. The ITF forms are widely appreciated for their traditional qualities, aesthetic beauty, and technical variety. According to Choi, the 24 patterns are meant to represent 24 hours, one

day, or all of one's life, and are a metaphor for the idea that the life of a human being is but a day, when compared to the life of the universe.

Hyŏng, P'umsae, or T'ŭl?

Today, there are three common Korean terms used to refer to "forms." They are Hyŏng, P'umsae, or T'ŭl. The term used varies by style or federation and is mostly a reflection of their attempt to differentiate themselves from each other or foreign influences. It is not a reflection of any fundamental difference in how these organizations conceptualize forms training. Hyŏng ("form" or "pattern"), a Sino-Korean term, is likely the oldest. P'um-sae ("shape of motions") is a Korean coined-word. T'ŭl ("pattern") is a term adopted by the ITF, which replaced their earlier use of the word Hyŏng.

Forms in this Book

The first form in each colored-belt system (P'algwae, T'aegŭk, and ITF) is shown on the following pages. In author's 896-page Taekwondo book, 250-plus pages provide an in depth overview of the 49 forms previously outlined, as well as general principles, summary charts, rank requirements, and an overview of the historical and philosophical meanings associated with each form.

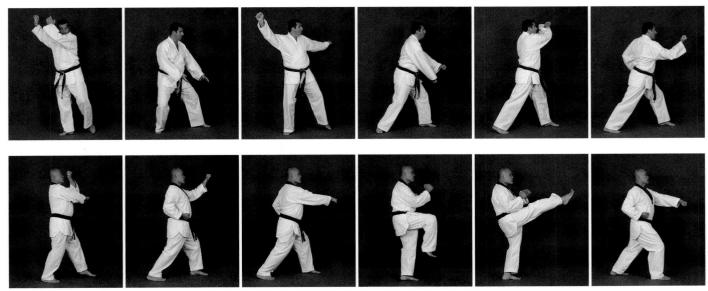

Top: long traditional motions as typified in ITF forms (a portion of Toi Gye is shown). Bottom: short modern motions as typified in T'aegŭk forms (a portion of T'aegŭk 6 is shown).

O	Attention, assume Basic Ready Stance Announce the form: "P'algwae il Chang"	11	R foot steps 180° cw into R Back Stance R Outside Knife Block (middle)
1	L foot steps 90° left into L Front Stance L Low Block	12	L foot steps forward into L Back Stance L Inside Block (middle)
2	R foot steps forward into R Front Stance R Inside Block (middle)	13	L foot steps 90° left into L Front Stance L Low Block
3	R foot steps 180° cw into R Front Stance R Low Block	14	R foot steps forward into R Front Stance R Inside Knife Hand Strike to neck
4	L foot steps forward into L Front Stance L Inside Block (middle)	15	L foot steps forward into L Front Stance L Inside Knife Hand Strike to neck
5	L foot steps 90° left into L Front Stance L Low Block	16 *	R foot steps forward into R Front Stance R Lunge Punch (middle), Kihap
6	R foot steps forward into R Back Stance R Inside Block (middle)	17	L foot steps 270° ccw into L Front Stance L Low Block
7	L foot steps forward into L Back Stance L Inside Block (middle)	18	R foot steps forward into R Front Stance R Inside Block (middle)
8 *	R foot steps forward into R Front Stance R Lunge Punch (middle), Kihap	19	R foot steps 180° cw into R Front Stance R Low Block
9	L foot steps 270° ccw to L Back Stance L Outside Knife Block (middle)	20	L foot steps forward into L Front Stance L Inside Block (middle)
10	R foot steps forward into R Back Stance R Inside Block (middle)	O	L foot steps back behind R foot, turn 90° left, assume Basic Ready Stance

Normal

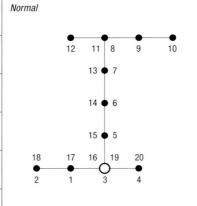

Reverse

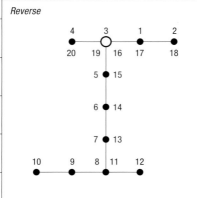

Footwork for 3, 11, and 20
(reverse view)

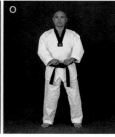

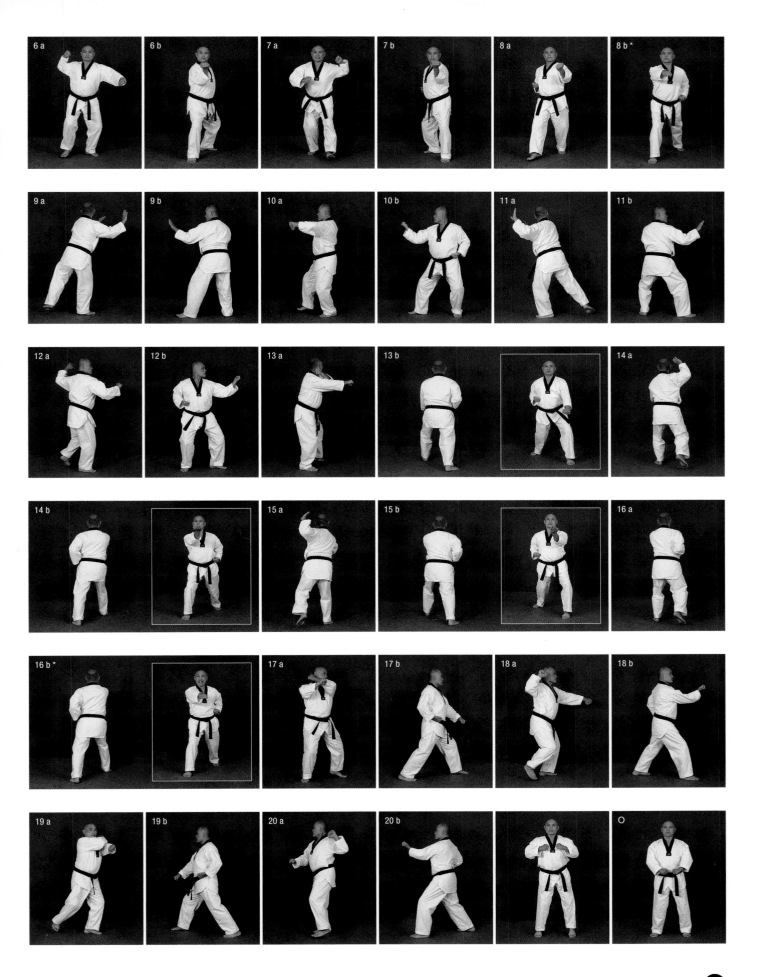

O	Attention, assume Basic Ready Stance Announce the form: "T'aegŭk il Chang"	11	R foot steps 90° right into R Front Stance R Low Block
1	L foot steps 90° left into L Walking Stance L Low Block	12	Maintain previous stance L Reverse Punch (middle)
2	R foot steps forward into R Walking Stance R Lunge Punch (middle)	13	L foot steps 90° left into L Walking Stance L Rising Block
3	R foot steps 180° cw into R Walking Stance R Low Block	14	1) R Front Kick (middle), into R Walking Stance 2) R Lunge Punch (middle)
4	L foot steps forward into L Walking Stance L Lunge Punch (middle)	15	R foot steps 180° cw into R Walking Stance R Rising Block
5	L foot steps 90° left into L Front Stance L Low Block	16	1) L Front Kick (middle), into L Walking Stance 2) L Lunge Punch (middle)
6	Maintain previous stance R Reverse Punch (middle)	17	L foot steps 90° right into L Front Stance L Low Block
7	R foot steps 90° right into R Walking Stance L Inside Block (middle)	18 *	R foot steps forward into R Front Stance R Lunge Punch (middle), Kihap
8	L foot steps forward into L Walking Stance R Reverse Punch (middle)	O	L foot steps 180° ccw, assume Basic Ready Stance
9	L foot steps 180° ccw into L Walking Stance R Inside Block (middle)		
10	R foot steps forward into R Walking Stance L Reverse Punch (middle)		

Normal

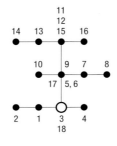

Reverse

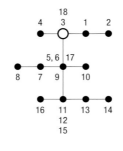

Notes Pertaining to all T'aegŭk Forms:

When compared to the P'algwae forms, most of the T'aegŭk forms are generally characterized by shorter, quicker deliveries, which are intended to be more modern. When assuming a *Ready Stance*, most practitioners do not rise onto the balls of their feet (feet remain planted), and the hands are not lifted as high before being lowered to waist level (see, O at end of this form). When executing a *Low Block* (5b), note that the fist finishes aligned with the groin. In P'algwae forms, historically the fist is aligned with the thigh (see P'algwae 1, 5b).

There are other subtle distinctions, best grasped by training with a qualified instructor and carefully observing the photos. Generally, many of the distinctions that characterize T'aegŭk forms are said to be more modern and more Korean-influenced, although this is debatable.

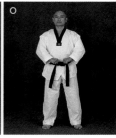

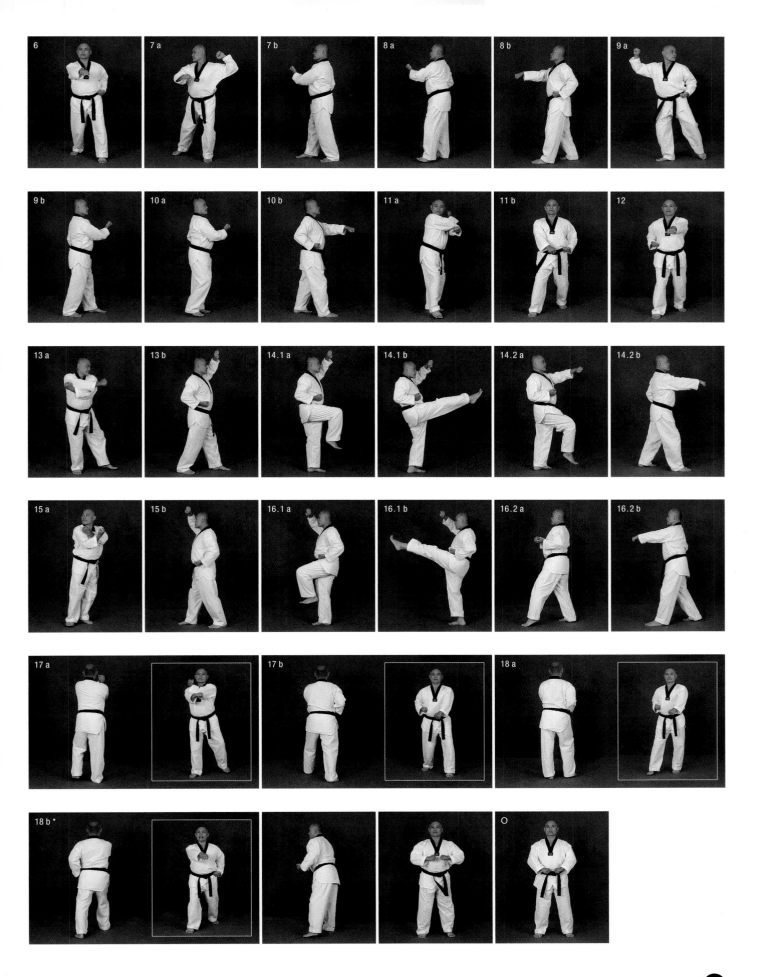

O	Attention, assume Basic Ready Stance Announce the form: "Ch'ŏn Ji"	11	R foot steps 180° cw into R Back Stance R Outside Block (middle)
1	L foot steps 90° left into L Front Stance L Low Block	12	L foot steps forward into L Front Stance L Lunge Punch (middle)
2	R foot steps forward into R Front Stance R Lunge Punch (middle)	13	L foot steps 90° left into L Back Stance L Outside Block (middle)
3	R foot steps 180° cw into R Front Stance R Low Block	14	R foot steps forward into R Front Stance R Lunge Punch (middle)
4	L foot steps forward into L Front Stance L Lunge Punch (middle)	15	R foot steps 180° cw into R Back Stance R Outside Block (middle)
5	L foot steps 90° left into L Front Stance L Low Block	16	L foot steps forward into L Front Stance L Lunge Punch (middle)
6	R foot steps forward into R Front Stance R Lunge Punch (middle)	17	R foot steps forward into R Front Stance R Lunge Punch (middle)
7	R foot steps 180° cw into R Front Stance R Low Block	18	R foot steps backward into L Front Stance L Lunge Punch (middle)
8	L foot steps forward into L Front Stance L Lunge Punch (middle)	19	L foot steps backward into R Front Stance R Lunge Punch (middle)
9	L foot steps 90° left into L Back Stance L Outside Block (middle)	O	L foot steps forward, even with R foot, assume Basic Ready Stance
10	R foot steps forward into R Front Stance R Lunge Punch (middle)		

Normal

```
                17 ● 6

                16 ● 5

 2     1    3, 18 7    4      10
 ●─────●──────○──────●──────●
      12   15 11    9    10

              13, 19 ● 8

                14 ●
```

Reverse

```
                    ● 14

              8 ●  13, 19

 10     9   11│15    12
 ●─────●──────○──────●──────●
      4    7│3, 18 1      2

              5 ● 16

              6 ● 17
```

*Footwork for 1–3 and 10
(reverse view)*

Notes Pertaining to all ITF Patterns:

When compared to the P'algwae, T'aegŭk, and WTF Black Belt forms, ITF patterns are distinctly different, and are most notably distinguished by: longer deliveries, greater use of circular motions, different chambering and delivery motions for some strikes and blocks, and a distinct, rhythmic rising and sinking of the body as one moves between techniques (see "Wave Motion" in the *Movement* chapter of the author's 896-page Taekwondo book). The subtleties that characterize ITF patterns are often difficult to perceive in still photography, and are best grasped by training with a qualified instructor. Note that the target height indicated by strikes and blocks (high, middle, low) is articulated slightly differently when compared to the previous forms. For example, ITF low strikes are executed at your navel level (instead of the groin), and middle strikes at your shoulder level (instead of the solar plexus)—the idea being that your body drops lower than your opponent's (raising their targets relative to yours). Middle blocks also tend to be higher for this reason. The Kihaps (shouts) that originally punctuated key actions in ITF forms were later deleted by Hong-Hi Choi, the creator of these patterns, since he felt all actions are equally important.

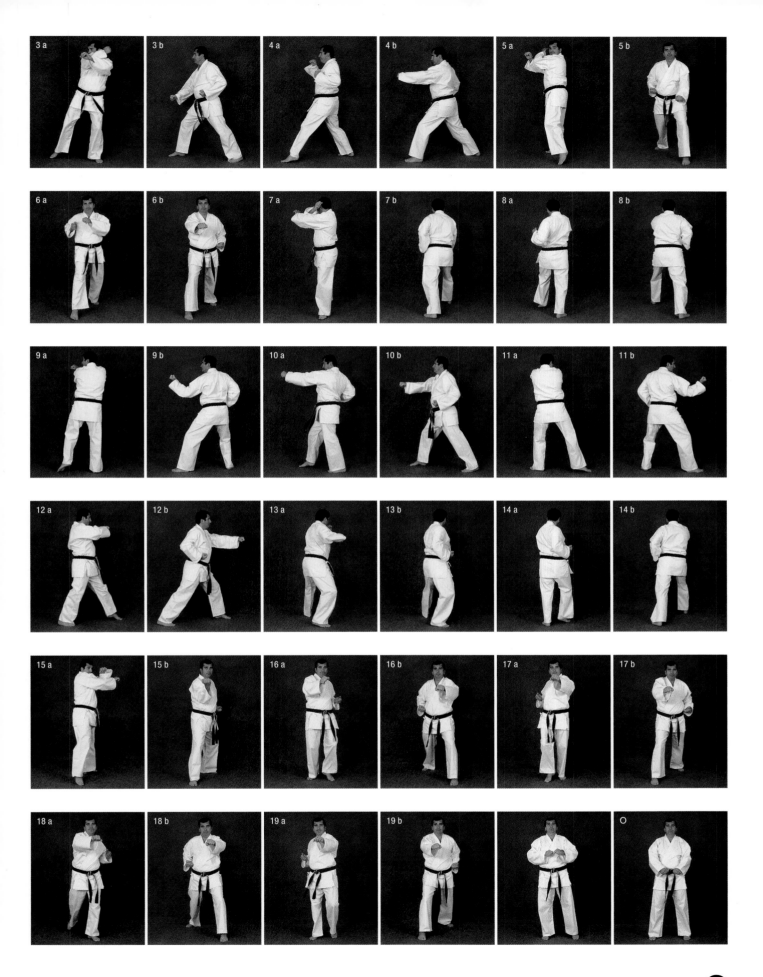

R E F E R E N C E

PROMOTION REQUIREMENTS

Summary

Expertise in specific technical areas is required for promotion to specific Taekwondo black belt ranks. Currently, actual promotion requirements vary widely by school and federation. Generally, skills evaluation occurs in four areas:

- Fundamental Skills
- Sparring
- Breaking
- Forms

Areas of evaluation are further broken down at right, according to rank. Note that colored-belt requirements are included in the listing for 1st Degree Black Belt. Schools that are competition oriented also base rank promotion on an athlete's performance in sport competition (sparring or forms).

Forms Requirements
Required forms vary by school and federation. A summary of forms, including the specific belt ranks associated with each, is found in the author's 896-page Taekwondo book, in the *Forms Overview* chapter, under "Forms Summary."

1st Degree Black Belt
Basic Knowledge
  History
  Philosophy
  Terminology
  Etiquette
  Class Procedures
  Vital Targets
Breathing + Meditation Skills
Leg Strikes
Hand Strikes
Three-Step Sparring
Two-Step Sparring
One-Step Sparring
Free Sparring
Self-Defense Sparring
Breaking
Forms
Written Essay
Moral Character

2nd Degree Black Belt
Advanced Jump Kicks
Jump Hand Strikes
Free Sparring
Self-Defense Sparring
Breaking
Forms
Written Essay
Teaching Experience
Competition Experience
Moral Character

3rd Degree Black
Advanced Jump Kicks
Free Sparring
Self-Defense Sparring
Breaking
Forms
Written Essay
Teaching Experience
Competition Experience
Moral Character

4th Degree Black Belt
Mastery of 1st–3rd Degree Black Belt skills
Comprehensive Knowledge
  History
  Philosophy
Technical Virtuosity (in all areas)
Advanced Jump Kicks
Free Sparring
Self-Defense Sparring
Breaking
Forms
Written Essay
Teaching Experience
Competition Experience
Contributions to Taekwondo
Moral Character

5th to 9th Degree Black Belt
Depending on the system, skill testing usually ends at 4th degree black belt, after which promotion is based on continued mastery of technical skills, years of service, and contributions to the art of Taekwondo. In some systems, candidates for advanced ranks are also evaluated in the following areas:

Forms
Breaking
Written Thesis
Teaching History
Quality of One's Students
Long-Term Impact on Taekwondo
Contributions to Society

Taekwondo Ranks

Rank [1]	Korean Name	Belt Color [1]	Min. Term [2]	Total Training [3]
10th Grade	10th Kŭp	White	2 months	none
9th Grade	9th Kŭp	White with stripe	2 months	2 months
8th Grade	8th Kŭp	Yellow	2 months	4 months
7th Grade	7th Kŭp	Yellow with stripe	2 months	6 months
6th Grade	6th Kŭp	Green	2 months	8 months
5th Grade	5th Kŭp	Green with stripe	2 months	10 months
4th Grade	4th Kŭp	Blue	2 months	1 year
3rd Grade	3rd Kŭp	Blue with stripe	2 months	14 months
2nd Grade	2nd Kŭp	Red	4 months	16 months
1st Grade	1st Kŭp	Red with stripe	4 months	20 months
1st Degree	Cho Dan	Black	1 year	2 years
2nd Degree	I Dan	Black	2 years	3 years
3rd Degree	Sam Dan	Black	3 years	5 years
4th Degree	Sa Dan	Black	4 years	8 years
5th Degree	O Dan	Black	5 years	12 years
6th Degree	Yuk Dan	Black	6 years	17 years
7th Degree	Ch'il Dan	Black	7 years	23 years
8th Degree	P'al Dan	Black	8 years	30 years
9th Degree	Ku Dan	Black	9 years	38 years

1) Color-belt systems currently in use vary widely by school and federation. Some systems use more colors; others use the system above but omit green. Some schools use a nine-grade system. In some systems, black belt ranks are indicated by the number of bars found at the end of one's black belt. Some practitioners feel this lacks modesty and so will not use bars to signify rank.

2) Minimum Term is the minimum time that must be spent at a given rank, before promotion to next higher rank. All time values given in this chart are based on 40 hours of training time per month. Thus, training for an hour per week for 2 years, is not the same as 10 hours per week for 2 years. In the United States, the average training time to 1st Degree Black Belt is 3 to 4 years.

3) Total Training is the total minimum training time that must be invested to achieve the given rank. For example, a holder of the First Degree will have trained for 2 years minimum.

Note: the information in this chart is based on averages and may vary by school or federation.

KOREAN TERMS

Basic Terms

Uniform	To-bok
Martial Art School	To-jang
National Flag	Kuk-ki
Korea	Han-guk
Instructor	Sa-bŏm
Instructor, Sir	Sa-bŏm-nim
Master	Kwan-jang
Master, Sir	Kwan-jang-nim
Thank you	Kam-sa ham-ni-da
Hello	An-nyŏng ha-shim-ni-kka
Goodbye (to person leaving)	An-nyŏng hi ka-ship-si-yo
Goodbye (to person staying)	An-nyŏng hi kye-ship-si-yo
Art, Method	Sul
Martial Arts	Mu-sul
Warrior	Mu-sa
Self-Defense	Ho-shin
Competition (sport)	Shi-hap
Form	P'um-se / P'um-sae / Hyŏng*
Pattern	T'ŭl
Energy-Harmonizing	Ki-hap
Energy-Shout	Ki-hap
External Power	Wae-gi
Internal Power	Nae-gi
Body (physical)	Shin-ch'e / Mom
Mind	Ma-ŭm
Spirit	Chŏng-shin
Philosophy	Ch'ŏl-hak

Training Commands

Attention	Ch'a-ryŏt
Bow to Flags	Kuk-ki e kyŏng-nye
Kneeling Position	Chŏng-jwa
Meditation	Mong-nyŏm
Return	Pa-ro
Bow	Kyŏng-nye
Relax	Shwi-ŏ
Dismiss	Hae-san

Sparring Terms

Sparring	Kyŏ-ru-gi
Arranged Sparring	Mat-ch'wŏ kyŏ-ru-gi
Free Sparring	Cha-yu kyŏ-ru-gi
Attack	Kong-kyŏk
Protective Armor	Ho-gu
Attention	Ch'a-ryŏt
Bow	Kyŏng-nye
Ready	Chun-bi
Start	Shi-jak
Stop/Separate	Kal-lyŏ
Continue	Kye-sok
Stop/End	Kŭ-man
Bow	Kyŏng-nye
Winner	Sŭng
Decision	P'an-jŏng
Disqualification	Shil-kyŏk
Superiority	U-se
Judge	Shim-p'an (-sa)
Referee	Chu-shim

Counting	Native-Korean	Sino-Korean
One	Ha-na	il
Two	Tu(l)	i
Three	Se(t)	Sam
Four	Ne(t)	Sa
Five	Ta-sŏt	O
Six	Yo-sŏt	Yuk
Seven	il-gop	Ch'il
Eight	Yŏ-dŏl	P'al
Nine	A-hop	Ku
Ten	Yŏl	Ship

Colors

White	Ha-yan / Hŭin / Paek*
Yellow	No-rang / Hwang*
Orange	Kyul*
Green	Ch'o-rok*
Purple	Po-ra
Blue	P'a-rang / Ch'ŏng*
Red	Ppal-kkan / Hong*
Brown	Kal-saek
Black	Kka-man / Hŭk*

Strikes

Punch	Jji-rŭ-gi
Strike	Ch'i-gi
Lunge Punch	Pa-ro Jji-rŭ-gi
Reverse Punch	Pan-dae Jji-rŭ-gi
Hook Punch	Nak-ka Jji-rŭ-gi
Back Fist Strike	Tŭng Ju-mŏk Ch'i-gi
Hammer Fist Strike	Me Ju-mŏk Ch'i-gi
Knife Hand Strike	Son-nal Ch'i-gi
Ridge Hand Strike	Son-nal Tŭng Ch'i-gi
Spear Hand Strike	Son-kkŭt Jji-rŭ-gi
Elbow Strike	P'al-kŭp Ch'i-gi

Kicks

Kick	Ch'a-gi
Front Kick	Ap Ch'a-gi
Side Kick	Yŏp Ch'a-gi
Roundhouse Kick	Tol-lyŏ Ch'a-gi
Back Kick	Twi Ch'a-gi
Hook Kick	Nak-ka Ch'a-gi
Whip Kick	Hu-ryŏ Ch'a-gi
Downward Kick	Nae-ryŏ Ch'a-gi
Crescent Kick	Pan-dal Ch'a-gi
Knee Strike	Mu-rŭp Ch'i-gi

Blocks

Block	Mak-ki
Rising Block	Ol-lyŏ Mak-ki
Low Block	A-rae Mak-ki
Inside Block	An Mak-ki
Outside Block	Pa-kkat Mak-ki
Knife Block	Son-nal Mak-ki

* Sino-Korean derivation

FURTHER READING

Philosophy and Religion

Chan, Wing-Tsit, trans. and comp.
A Source Book in Chinese Philosophy.
Princeton NJ: Princeton University Press, 1963.

Earhart, Byron H, edit.
Religious Traditions of the World.
San Francisco: HarperCollins Publishers, 1993.

Smith, Huston.
The Illustrated World's Religions:
A Guide to Our Wisdom Traditions
San Francisco: HarperCollins Publishers, 1994.

Zimmer, Heinrich.
Philosophies of India.
Edited by Joseph Campbell.
Princeton NJ: Princeton University Press, 1969.

Medicine

Cohen, Kenneth S.
The Way of Qigong: The Art and Science
of Chinese Energy Healing.
New York: Ballantine Books, 1997.

Dox, Ida; John Melloni; and Gilbert Eisner.
The HarperCollins Illustrated Medical Dictionary.
New York: HarperCollins Publishers, 1993.

Kaptchuk, Ted J.
The Web That Has No Weaver:
Understanding Chinese Medicine.
New York: Congdon & Weed, 1983.

Maciocia, Giovanni.
The Foundations of Chinese Medicine.
London: Churchhill Livingston, 1989.

Netter, Frank H.
Atlas of Human Anatomy.
Summit NJ: Novartis Pharmaceuticals, 1989.

Tedeschi, Marc.
Essential Anatomy for Healing and Martial Arts.
New York: Weatherhill, 2000.
———. *Essential Acupoints.* (Poster)
New York: Weatherhill, 2002.

Van Alphen, Jan, and Anthony Aris, editors.
Oriental Medicine: An Illustrated Guide
to the Asian Arts of Healing.
Boston: Shambala Publications, 1997.

Martial Arts

Draeger, Donn F.
Classical Bujutsu: The Martial Arts and Ways of
Japan (Volume 1). New York: Weatherhill, 1973.
———. *Classical Budo: The Martial Arts and Ways*
of Japan (Volume 2). New York: Weatherhill, 1973.
———. *Modern Bujutsu & Budo: The Martial Arts*
and Ways of Japan (Volume 3). Weatherhill, 1974.

Draeger, Donn F., and Robert W. Smith.
Comprehensive Asian Fighting Arts.
New York: Kodansha, 1980.

Farkas, Emil, and John Corcoran.
Martial Arts: Traditions, History, People.
New York: Smith Publications, 1983.

Funakoshi, Gichin.
Karate-Do: My Way of Life.
Tokyo: Kodansha, 1975.

Haines, Bruce A.
Karate's History and Traditions.
Tokyo: Tuttle, 1968.

Kano, Jigoro.
Kodokan Judo.
Tokyo: Kodansha, 1986 (first published 1956).

Lee, Bruce.
Tao of Jeet Kune Do.
Santa Clarita, CA: Ohara Publications, 1975.

Nakayama, Masatoshi.
Dynamic Karate.
Tokyo: Kodansha, 1966.

Nelson, Randy F., edit.
The Overlook Martial Arts Reader:
Classic Writings on Philosophy and Technique.
Woodstock NY: Overlook Press, 1989.

Tedeschi, Marc.
The Art of Striking: Principles & Techniques.
New York: Weatherhill, 2002.
———. *The Art of Holding: Principles & Techniques.*
New York: Weatherhill, 2001.
———. *The Art of Throwing: Principles &*
Techniques. New York: Weatherhill, 2001.
———. *The Art of Ground Fighting: Principles &*
Techniques. New York: Weatherhill, 2002.
———. *The Art of Weapons: Armed and Unarmed*
Self-Defense. New York: Weatherhill, 2003.

Korean Martial Arts

Cho, Sihak H.
Taekwondo: Secrets of Korean Karate.
Tokyo: Tuttle, 1968.

Choi, Hong-Hi.
Encyclopedia of Taekwon-do. (15 volumes)
Canada: International Taekwon-Do
Federation, 1985.

Chun, Richard, and P.H. Wilson.
Tae Kwon Do: The Korean Martial Art.
New York: Harper & Row, 1976.

Hwang, Kee.
Tang Soo Do (Soo Bahk Do).
South Korea: Sung Moon Sa, 1978.

Kang, Won-Sik, and Kyong-Myong Lee.
A Modern History of Taekwondo.
Seoul: Bokyung Moonhwasa, 1999.

Kukkiwon, and Un-Yong Kim.
Taekwondo Textbook.
Seoul: Oh Sung, 1995.

Lee, Joo-Bang.
The Ancient Martial Art of Hwarangdo. (3 volumes)
Burbank CA: Ohara Publications, 1978.

Suh, In Hyuk, and Jane Hallander.
The Fighting Weapons of Korean Martial Arts.
Burbank CA: Unique Publications, 1988.

Tedeschi, Marc.
Hapkido: Traditions, Philosophy, Technique.
New York: Weatherhill, 2000.
———. *Taekwondo: Traditions, Philosophy,*
Technique. New York: Weatherhill, 2003.

Korean Art and Culture

McKillop, Beth.
Korean Art and Design.
New York: HarperCollins, 1992.

Storey, Robert.
Korea.
Australia: Lonely Planet, 1997.

Youngsook, Pak, edit.
Arts of Korea.
New York: Metropolitan Museum of Art, 1998.

"This book is in my experience the most comprehensive ever written on a single martial art. It is superbly organized, highly informative, and contains thousands of outstanding photographs. An authoritative presentation of basic principles and techniques, integrated with modern innovations, makes this work indispensable to martial artists of virtually any style."
— **PROFESSOR WALLY JAY**

"Within minutes of opening Marc Tedeschi's new book, *Hapkido*, you know you have your hands on an exceptional work. *Hapkido* is an enormous, comprehensive, detailed, beautifully illustrated and, somehow, very personal reference work for those who want to learn about this fascinating martial art. I predict it will soon be as much a part of the required-reading list for martial arts practitioners as are Donn Draeger's *The Martial Arts and Ways of Japan*, Eugen Herrigel's *Zen in the Art of Archery*, and Bruce Lee's *The Tao of Jeet Kune Do*. At the same time, Hapkido goes far above and beyond these books, and beyond almost any other martial arts reference work, by examining the traditions, philosophy, and techniques of hapkido with an astonishing degree of detail . . . It covers so much ground and its material is so well presented that no martial arts library will again be complete without it."
— **JOURNAL OF ASIAN MARTIAL ARTS**

"If you hold this book in your hand, words will fail you. 1136 pages, more than 9000 photos, 2.5 inches thick, 11 x 8.5 inches large, and almost 8 lbs heavy! If you turn to the first pages you are lost. You forget the time and you are lost in the apparently infinite information explosion contained in this work . . . for the Hapkidoin it is a treasure chest full of information and impulses . . . If I had the choice to take a book with me onto a lonely island, I would decide on this book . . . An absolute must for any Hapkidoin!"
— **HAPKIDOSHOP.COM**

"*Hapkido* is an overwhelming achievement. Its comprehensiveness and the quality of the writing and design are unmatched in martial arts literature. The author's integration of history, philosophy, and technique into the larger framework of martial arts as a whole makes this book invaluable to any martial artist. Tedeschi's treatment of weapons techniques is honest, practical, and well worth studying."
— **NICKLAUS SUINO**, author of *The Art of Japanese Swordsmanship*

☆☆☆☆☆ *An Encyclopedia of Hapkido and Martial Arts*
"This book is simply outstanding. The depth and volume of information provided is impressive to say the least. Presented in large format on quality paper, it covers the width and breadth of Hapkido. The overview contains interviews with all prominent grandmasters, including Yong-Sul Choi. An exhaustive list of techniques are illustrated with sequence photos and detailed descriptions. It covers everything from the basics to weapons and protecting others. As a bonus, it includes extensive acupressure diagrams and descriptions. It treats Hapkido as a science without losing its art form."
— **AMAZON.COM CUSTOMER REVIEW**

"I am impressed. This book is one extremely large, very nearly complete, reference on all aspects of Hapkido. I say "very nearly" not as a criticism, but in astonishment, simply because this book covers almost all of a huge curriculum. In addition to a huge technique reference section, it contains a number of interesting interviews, cool historical pictures, and a number of well-written chapters on many aspects of Hapkido not normally written about . . . the verbal [technical] descriptions are the best."
— **NEBRASKA HAPKIDO ASSOCIATION BOOKSTORE**

"Without a doubt the best works on martial arts today are those written by Marc Tedeschi . . . great reference for anyone who is serious about learning or teaching the martial arts."
— **PROFESSOR WILLY CAHILL**, Two-time Olympic Judo Coach

Taekwondo

Designed and illustrated by Marc Tedeschi.

Principal photography by Marc Tedeschi.

Contributing photography by Shelley Firth,

Frank Deras, or as noted by photographs.

Editorial supervision by Ray Furse.

Korean language editing by Patrick Chew.

Cover calligraphy by Monica Dengo.

Production consultation by Bill Rose.

The majority of the photographs were shot digitally

using Nikon cameras, and on Plus-X film

using Leica and Hasselblad cameras.

Digital-type composition and page layout originated

on an Apple Macintosh G4 computer.

Typeset in Helvetica Neue, Univers,

Sabon, Weiss, and Times.

Printed and bound by Oceanic Graphic Printing

and C&C Offset Printing in China.

Published and distributed by Weatherhill.

Weatherhill

PUBLISHERS OF FINE BOOKS ON
ASIA AND THE PACIFIC